for various academic experiences and in structuring the educational process itself. It argues that learning can and does take place in different ways for different people and that to continue to provide only one form of instruction wastes the country's intellectual resources.

Explorations in Non-Traditional Study provides information for colleges that are considering the pros and cons of non-traditional study. It is for administrators and educational planners who want to break the lockstep, accumulation-of-credits approach to education that prevents many people from receiving a recognized college education.

THE AUTHORS

SAMUEL B. GOULD is chancellor emeritus of the State University of New York and chancellor *pro tempore* of Connecticut Commission for Higher Education.

K. PATRICIA CROSS is senior research psychologist with the Educational Testing Service and research educator for the Center for Research and Development in Higher Education, University of California, Berkeley.

The other authors are identified in the front of the book.

Explorations in
Non-Traditional Study

Samuel B. Gould
K. Patricia Cross
Editors

Explorations in Non-Traditional Study

 Jossey-Bass Inc., Publishers
San Francisco • Washington • London • 1977

EXPLORATIONS IN NON-TRADITIONAL STUDY
Samuel B. Gould and K. Patricia Cross, Editors

LA
227.3
.Y66

JACKET DESIGN BY WILLI BAUM

FIRST EDITION
First printing: April 1972
Second printing: December 1972
Third printing: January 1977

Code 7212

The Jossey-Bass
Series in Higher Education

ᘜᘜᘜᘜᘜᘜᘜᘜᘜᘜᘜᘜᘜᘜᘜᘜᘜᘜ

A publication of the
COMMISSION ON NON-TRADITIONAL STUDY
Samuel B. Gould, Chairman

Preface

It seems quite clear to members of the Commission on Non-Traditional Study that educators and laymen, who more and more are considering the pros and cons of non-traditional study, need as much knowledge about it as can be made available. Hence, we are trying, through the background material presented here and through other Commission publications, to help those concerned with the future of postsecondary education toward a broad understanding of the important issues involved. *Explorations in Non-Traditional Study* is an outgrowth of the first probes of the Commission and is a cooperative effort of Commission members and staff. It is in no way a presentation of final conclusions or recommendations since the chapters were prepared originally to assist the Commission in acquiring information and identifying issues.

Most people in the educational world probably know by now that the Commission is sponsored jointly by the College Entrance Examination Board and Educational Testing Service. It is financed primarily by a two-year grant from the Carnegie Corporation. The first of these two years is now over, and the Commission is moving steadily toward evaluating its findings and making broad recommendations for further action by appropriate and permanent bodies.

Six Commission subcommittees examined several basic elements of non-traditional study: the concepts underlying it, the kinds of access to postsecondary education that should exist, the means by which such education might take place, the models of non-traditional education that are in operation or being planned, the recognition of or reward for educational work completed in non-traditional ways, and the problems of finance involved. The subcommittees worked diligently and presented preliminary reports to the full Commission. Four of these are included in *Explorations in Non-Traditional Study*. The findings and recommendations of the means and finance subcommittees will be reflected in other ways as the Commission continues its work.

During 1971 the full Commission met three times: in March to organize itself and its tasks; in July to examine and discuss preliminary findings of the subcommittees as well as to reassess objectives and regroup forces; in November to discuss in some depth several basic issues and to hear presentations describing representative models of non-traditional study that are in either operational or planning stages. Individuals directly involved in developing these new programs reported their plans, problems, and progress to date. Representatives of fifty educational agencies or organizations were invited to attend that meeting, which was held in Washington, D.C. Most of them accepted and contributed a great deal through their questions and comments.

During the winter and spring of 1972, Commission members met several times in special sessions with representatives of various segments of the educational community that affect and are affected by non-traditional study. Present plans call for a meeting of the full Commission in June 1972 and completion of a draft of its final report by the fall of 1972. In early winter of 1973, the Commission will hold an invitational

Preface

conference, where its final report will serve as the springboard for a discussion of the findings and their significance.

On the publication side, *Explorations in Non-Traditional Study* will be followed by a comprehensive treatment of the external degree, which has emerged as a major element of non-traditional study. It will be available by the summer of 1972. The final report will be published as soon as possible after the 1973 winter conference.

In addition, the Commission, realizing how incomplete and inconclusive present data are in virtually all aspects of non-traditional study, is engaged in preparing a comprehensive research plan for gathering the hard information needed if non-traditional study is to develop effectively. We hope that such a research map will lead to specific studies that will yield some data before the completion of our report and therefore have influence on it.

The authors of the chapters in *Explorations in Non-Traditional Study,* singly and collectively, have performed a difficult but essential service, and we are grateful to them. The administrative staff work of Jane Wirsig was a key factor in the emergence of material broad enough in approach, yet detailed enough as well, to form appropriate background information about non-traditional approaches to education. John Valentine, executive secretary of the Commission, and Florence Kiey, its executive assistant, were also very much involved in the preparatory steps that led to this book.

We express our special thanks to these people and reiterate our appreciation to the Commission members, staff, sponsors, and the Carnegie Corporation for making possible the steady movement of the Commission toward the goals it has set.

Princeton   SAMUEL B. GOULD
Berkeley   K. PATRICIA CROSS
January 1972

Commission
Members

SAMUEL B. GOULD (chairman), *chancellor emeritus of the State University of New York and chancellor* pro tempore *of Connecticut Commission on Higher Education*

M. ROBERT ALLEN, *dean, Division of Continuing Education, University of Miami.*

HOWARD R. BOWEN, *chancellor, Claremont University Center*

MARY I. BUNTING, *president, Radcliffe College*

HENRY CHAUNCEY, *president, Interuniversity Communications Council, Inc.* (*EDUCOM*)

Members of the Commission

ARLAND F. CHRIST-JANER, *president, College Entrance Examination Board (ex officio)*

FRED C. COLE, *president, Council on Library Resources*

JOSEPH P. COSAND, *deputy commissioner for higher education, United States Office of Education*

BERTRAM H. DAVIS, *general secretary, American Association of University Professors*

WALTER G. DAVIS, *director, Department of Education, American Federation of Labor–Congress of Industrial Organizations*

FRANK G. DICKEY, *executive director, National Commission on Accrediting*

W. TODD FURNISS, *director, Commission on Academic Affairs, American Council on Education*

RICHARD C. GILMAN, *president, Occidental College*

CYRIL O. HOULE, *professor of education, University of Chicago*

C. ALBERT KOOB, *president, National Catholic Educational Association*

ELIZABETH D. KOONTZ, *director, Women's Bureau, United States Department of Labor*

CHARLES A. LeMAISTRE, *chancellor, The University of Texas System*

JOHN W. MACY, JR., *president, Corporation for Public Broadcasting*

Members of the Commission

Subcommittee Members

CONCEPTS

W. TODD FURNISS, Chairman
JAMES A. PERKINS
STEPHEN H. SPURR
WILLIAM W. TURNBULL

Staff:

RODNEY T. HARTNETT*
CAROLE A. LELAND**

ACCESS

LELAND L. MEDSKER,
    Chairman
MARY I. BUNTING
ARLAND F. CHRIST-JANER
WALTER G. DAVIS
ELIZABETH D. KOONTZ

Staff:

K. PATRICIA CROSS*
J. QUENTIN JONES**

Members of the Subcommittees

MEANS

JAMES PARTON, Chairman
HENRY CHAUNCEY
FRED C. COLE
JOHN W. MACY, JR.

Staff:
ELDON PARK*
FRANCES C. THOMSON**
WESLEY W. WALTON*

MODELS

CYRIL O. HOULE,
    Chairman
M. ROBERT ALLEN
CHARLES A. LEMAISTRE
FELIX C. ROBB

Staff:
GEORGE H. HANFORD**
JOHN R. VALLEY*

RECOGNITION

FRANK G. DICKEY,
    Chairman
JOSEPH P. COSAND
BERTRAM H. DAVIS
RICHARD C. GILMAN
CLIFTON R. WHARTON, JR.

Staff:
JACK N. ARBOLINO**
ERNEST W. KIMMEL*

FINANCE

HOWARD R. BOWEN,
    Chairman
C. ALBERT KOOB
ALICE RIVLIN

Staff:
DAVID J. BRODSKY*
MERRITT LUDWIG**
JOHN M. MULLINS**

  * *Educational Testing Service*
 ** *College Entrance Examination Board*

Contents

Contents

Explorations in Non-Traditional Study

Background essays prepared for the
COMMISSION ON NON-TRADITIONAL STUDY
888 Seventh Avenue, New York 10019

Prologue

Samuel B. Gould

Prospects for Non-Traditional Study

𝄟𝄟𝄟𝄟𝄟𝄟𝄟𝄟𝄟𝄟𝄟𝄟𝄟𝄟𝄟𝄟𝄟𝄟𝄟𝄟𝄟

Non-traditional study may be defined in simplest terms as a group of changing educational patterns caused by the changing needs and opportunities of society. Much of it is not new. Indeed, there have always been non-traditional approaches to education in one place or another, some of them very successful. But current perceptions of the needs of new and hitherto unserved segments of our population, together with strong dissatisfactions with results from those segments traditionally served, have now catapulted non-traditional study to the forefront of public attention. It has suddenly been discovered by federal and state government agencies, as well as by individuals in and outside the academic world. And, as might naturally be expected, it is already surrounded with considerable confusion, not only about what it is but about what it can be expected to do.

The Commission on Non-Traditional Study came into being as a response to this general confusion. Its sponsors and the Carnegie Corporation believed that, in the public interest, such a commission was necessary to take a careful and independent look at what is evolving, to make some judgments and evaluations, and eventually to offer some recommendations for the future.

As the Preface makes clear, this book presents a set of preliminary working papers that explore some of the issues involved in non-traditional study. No conclusions or recommendations of the Commission are included. These will come later and will occasion, I hope, an open and constructive debate as non-traditional study impinges more and more on the national consciousness.

The Commission has limited its purview to examining postsecondary education. This limitation does not mean, however, that non-traditional study should be confined to that level. Education should be a continuum without the sorts of carefully segmented portions to which we are accustomed. We all know what this segmentation can do in confusing the student as he passes from one level to another. We know also the dangerous and debilitating caste system among teachers which has resulted from years of such careful separation. But as we think about non-traditional approaches, we realize that a student nurtured in traditional forms of education at the elementary and secondary levels may have great difficulty when suddenly confronted with non-traditional options that give him more flexibility, more independence, and more responsibilities for self-motivation.

Non-traditional methods should be at least partially familiar to the student from his earliest educational experiences and should be more and more in his consciousness as he grows older. Much of a non-traditional nature has already been done at the elementary and secondary levels, and much more deserves to be contemplated. The problems are different but nonetheless important. They involve, above all, the development of student and teacher attitudes receptive to the unorthodox approaches encompassed in the non-traditional concept and the development of student and teacher abilities to cope with such approaches.

In this Prologue, I want to identify some patterns that characterize non-traditional education as it is currently perceived, applying them to higher education but not necessarily limiting them to that level. In one way or another, the chapters that follow elaborate on various aspects of these patterns and deal more specifically with the philosophy and approaches of non-traditional study as it is developing in this country.

The major patterns have to do with four general areas, and far less is known about all of them than needs to be. We can identify them much more easily than we can offer full explanations or documented detail, yet for our present purposes even their identification and our current knowledge may be helpful.

The first set of patterns is woven around the philosophy of full educational opportunity. Its goal is to assure each individual, regardless of age, previous formal education, or circumstances of life, the amount and type of education that will add to and develop his potential as a person. This is a democratic philosophy, in keeping with the principles on which the United States has developed as a nation.

In these times particularly, with much dissatisfaction expressed about habits, attitudes, actions, and moral values of the younger generation coupled with a new era of financial stringency for education, numerous voices call for a return to elitism—or at least to a much higher degree of student selectivity. Serious questions are being asked about who should be educated and why. In the course of this protest and questioning, all sorts of uncertainties are emerging, even about the precise definition of full opportunity. These confusions will have to be eliminated and a clear basis established from which future planning can proceed.

Within this pattern of full opportunity are a number of specific strands, all of which make new demands on the educational structure. There is, for example, the need to accommodate segments of our population as yet largely ignored— women who wish to resume their studies when their family and household duties permit, returning war veterans, retired men and women, inmates of penal institutions, employed people who wish to improve their situations, professionals or paraprofessionals who find they must keep up to date—a widely diversified group who seek in some fairly systematic way to enrich their lives. There is the enormous problem of the minorities, whose promise and opportunities are still unfulfilled. There is the need to reexamine vocational education: its availability, its methods, its goals, its relation to manpower use in this country. There is the sudden turning of attention to the so-called external degree, with its popular appeal and its latent dangers. There is even the current move toward exploration of a whole new kind of higher education system, apart from the traditional institutions now in existence, either to parallel what we now have or to replace it almost completely. All these needs and pressures stem from the mood of democratization, from insistence that great additional numbers must be served, that full opportunity to rise on the educational scale must somehow be provided.

The second set of patterns emerges logically from the first. It includes elements of structure, method, content, and procedures that combine to create a new flexibility in education. Non-traditional study seeks to loosen the present rigidities in learning, not only because there has been opposition to them and sometimes even revolt against them, but because seemingly immutable truths about the learning process are suddenly being questioned seriously.

For example, the interruption of study during the formal years of education was until recently considered unfortunate; indeed, it even had a certain stigma attached to it. Now educators are having second thoughts. Some evidence indicates that in many cases and under certain circumstances such interruptions are beneficial rather than harmful. They add a maturing dimension that can have great and enduring value. And there is a wide variety of possible worthwhile interruptions.

Residential requirements of the most rigid sort were once invariably part of the degree-granting pattern. Life in the residence hall was unquestioned as an educational advantage. But now we are not quite so certain, even though we have a good deal of nostalgia about such a life style. All sorts of new forces have entered the picture—physical, psychological, social. And so we do not adhere quite so steadfastly to the proposition that residence on campus is philosophically or educationally desirable in every case. Our doubts are leading us to different and less traditional concepts about the values of campus residences, the kinds of institutions that need them, and the kinds of students who would benefit from inhabiting them.

Conventional subject matter and conventional instruction methods are similarly feeling pressures generated by those who rebel against their time-honored inflexibility. In both

5

instances non-traditional study offers new attractions. It can move readily into less compartmentalized explorations of knowledge and into movements of human change and growth. It can speed up, intensify, and be more relevant to today's learning process by using all the new electronic and other forms of instruction either already in existence or contemplated. Whether all these changes in subject matter and method are attractions or distractions is still the basis for considerable debate in educational circles, but everyone would probably agree that their impact is being felt in no small way.

Consideration of work experience as a component of education is still another aspect of the pattern of flexibility. There are two types to be identified: first, work and study as a regular curricular approach in college or university, and second, recognition of certain kinds of experience as being educationally valuable and therefore worthy of credit toward a degree. The former is a well-accepted academic adaptation presently being used, with variations in its details, by a few hundred of our higher education institutions; the latter is much less prevalent as an accepted concept or as an accepted part of the degree-granting process. Some proponents of non-traditional education are calling new attention to this concept and are urging that it be part of the total flexible pattern, assuming, of course, that such work experience would be carefully evaluated before academic credits were given.

A third set of patterns relates to the new or expanded educational roles being assumed by business, industry, labor unions, cultural, governmental, and social agencies, military commands, proprietary schools, correspondence institutes, and others. Together they form the sort of parallel education system I mentioned earlier, a system thus far having little contact with traditional institutions and, through its individual parts, pressing for degree-granting authority. This lack of contact could lead to duplicate and wasteful activities on the part of

6

every institution or agency, traditional or non-traditional. One thing is certain: A parallel system is bound to affect the traditional establishment in many ways, some that could be to the latter's advantage and some that in specific instances could destroy it. At this point many traditional educators and administrators and trustees are unaware that such a huge potential competitor exists. To quote myself for a moment (from *Today's Academic Condition,* McGraw-Hill, 1970, pp. 43–46):

> One of the most overlooked but powerful facts of our time is that we have come to a stage in our educational development where a good deal of what man learns, or *can* learn, is not a part of the formal educational system at all. . . . Americans are in an almost continuous state of perceiving, viewing all kinds of television programs many hours each week, reading books and periodicals of all kinds by the billion each year, buying millions of dollars worth of phonograph records and tapes, being bombarded day and night with impressions and messages. . . . Accordingly, we now observe a new phenomenon of educational life. We see publishing houses, electronics industries, commercial film makers, and others entering the field of knowledge dissemination competitively. Furthermore, we see them doing this occasionally with more skill and sophistication, with more of a sense of how learning takes place, than those who have for generations professed to be masters of the learning process.

The final set of patterns concerns individualized learning. There are two elements in this: individualized opportunity, whereby each student searches for the kind of education suitable and necessary for himself, and individualized responsibility, whereby each student, having decided on his educational goal and course of action, documents his motivation by satisfactory progress toward his goal. Our more traditional institutions do little, or at least not enough, to encourage this individualized approach. As a result they are sometimes populated to a considerable degree by students who have no appropriate reasons for being there while others are being rejected. Too many students are content to give themselves over to long-established classroom routines or subject matter because their reasons for attending are not particularly educational. Present high rates of attrition show clearly how often students are ill-chosen and ill-matched to the institutions they inhabit and how we are wasting our financial resources and misjudging our human ones.

If flexibility is a necessity for non-traditional study, then individualized learning is its most important component. It is an enormous step forward in breaking all sorts of lock-steps and in establishing for each person a set of educational directions that can take him where he, himself, needs to go. Individualized learning has many implications that are still rather mysterious, whether one thinks of selection, guidance, study patterns, rewards, or financial requirements both for the student and the institution. Without individualized learning non-traditional study becomes no more than a shadow of what it might be.

To speak of a shadow is to be reminded that much more than the shadow of a doubt hovers over non-traditional forms of education. There is doubt of considerable magnitude and in many quarters about the philosophical rightness, the validity, and especially the educational efficacy of such forms. The greatest doubt of all, a doubt coupled with outright disbelief, is centered on whether a set of patterns for non-traditional study can be created that will guarantee high quality in education rather than dilute it. The terms *external degree* or

Samuel B. Gould

individualized learning or *patterns of flexibility* have a suspiciously permissive ring, especially in the ears of traditionalist educators and a host of laymen as well, who consider current philosophies and practices of colleges and universities already too liberalized and weakened. They hear these terms and others, and they are convinced that every vestige of intellectual rigor will disappear into oblivion if the non-traditionalists gain any significant control of higher education. They sense a further proliferation of degree-granting under dubious auspices and with dubious requirements. They interpret individualized learning as individualized isolation, especially from faculty, and they look on flexibility as no more than a synonym for escape from regulation and responsibility.

These doubts and fears are sometimes justified and sometimes not, but they will continue unless and until non-traditional education develops a set of patterns specifically designed to counteract them. If some order is to emerge out of today's efforts—most of them well-intentioned, a certain number of them effective in and of themselves, practically all of them unilateral in concept and therefore limited—if we are not to have confusion verging on chaos as everyone proceeds in his own non-traditional fashion, if quality is indeed to be protected, then some very specific needs become apparent. Three developments are central: evaluation of individual capability and recognition of achievement, evaluation and accreditation of programs wherever they are created and promulgated, and safeguards for the protection and encouragement of human academic relationships in the midst of independent and often isolated circumstances of study.

The Commission on Non-Traditional Study has only begun to ponder these necessities, but it already sees that new agencies will have to be created to deal with such matters as evaluation and guidance, accreditation of programs, and recognition of individual achievement. The precise characteristics of

9

such agencies and their relationship to existing institutions remain to be determined as the Commission continues its work.

The Commission also sees the need to construct curricula that join non-traditional methods with regular student-faculty relationships, undoubtedly of a new type but more than ever essential. Its vision is not yet clear on all these issues, but it recognizes that until some plans can be formulated that tie many institutions and agencies together in a sharing of responsibility, much of what happens from now on will be duplicative, financially and educationally wasteful, and sometimes even dangerous to the future of higher education.

Similarly, the final set of patterns to be created is presently no more than a combination of unsolved problems—and will continue to be until some major research is undertaken. We must investigate how non-traditional study will be financed, what its costs are likely to be, whether these costs indicate paths to more economical or more expensive operation, what roles federal, state, or local governments, as well as private foundations, may be expected to play, what special effects there may be on private colleges and universities—a series of unanswered questions and issues about which conclusions must be reached. Models of non-traditional study now in operation will offer clues, but few models have existed long enough to give us more than anecdotal knowledge. And it is too early even to guess whether any unorthodox approaches to higher education will help to ease today's stringent financial circumstances.

We can be certain about a few prospects for non-traditional study. The first is that it will continue to develop and grow in this country whether or not it is carefully planned with appropriate evaluations and safeguards. Many Americans want it, they will search for where they can find it, and they will apply great pressure to bring it into being where it does

10

not yet exist. There is no blinking at this fact; it is the first reality the Commission discovered.

Another reality is that while little definitive knowledge has yet been gathered, a great body of mythology or folklore is emerging about non-traditional study. Some of this is positive, some negative. But it grows and grows, sometimes making this new form of education the answer to all of education's problems but just as frequently making it the object of suspicion or even condemnation. This condition will continue until experience and research substitute knowledge supported by data for wishful thinking influenced by prejudice.

The only other reality I can offer at this time is that so long as this nation continues to be a republic and fosters democratic ideals, the philosophy of full educational opportunity will spread and grow stronger. There will still be islands of elitism here and there, though not as many as there once were. The main thrust, however, already clearly evident, is toward total, lifelong opportunity with educational options in number and variety such as we of older generations never dreamed of or dared to hope for.

The prospects for non-traditional study are good. How soon they will be realized will depend, as so many other prospects in so many other areas of life have depended, on the will of the American people and the intelligence, balanced judgment, and ingenuity of those who are called upon to exercise it.

1

Rodney T. Hartnett

Non-Traditional
Study:
An Overview

𝄞𝄞𝄞𝄞𝄞𝄞𝄞𝄞𝄞𝄞𝄞𝄞𝄞𝄞𝄞𝄞𝄞

What is a college education? Who may legitimately claim to have one? The second question is easier to answer than the first. We know the pathways to obtaining a college degree; we know when the student has met the requirements; we even know what the degree will buy in terms of personal power and prestige. What we do not know, with any precision, are the characteristics and behaviors possessed by the educated person. Yet education is knowledge as well as process. There are pathways to knowledge other than the traditionally accepted four years of credit accumulation pursued by young people between the ages of 17 and 23 who devote essentially full time to formal classroom study. The challenge to higher education today is that of providing increased options and new educational opportunities to millions of people. The development of new options in learning requires careful examination of the concepts and criticisms of traditional education, as well as an analysis of the meaning, potential, and limitations of non-traditional alternatives.

What is meant by non-traditional study? Who needs it? How can it be evaluated? Is academic credit a necessary component in the recognition of educational achievement? If so, can credit be made flexible enough to accommodate diverse pathways to knowledge? Before non-traditional approaches can be considered viable, questions must be posed, discussions conducted, and alternatives proposed. Chapter One explores the concepts and limitations of traditional education, confronting present practices with new options. But non-traditional options, too, have both strengths and limitations.

If greater openness to evaluation and certification of diverse learning experiences is emphasized in non-traditional studies, do we then run the risk of substituting symbols—credits and degrees—for education itself? If non-traditional studies emphasize a broader conception of educational experiences, how can we differentiate valid educational experience from the learning experiences of life—such as traveling, working, or interacting with people? Who is responsible for maintaining standards of quality? Traditionalists have never contended that a college degree has uniform meaning across the broad diver-

sity of American higher education. Nevertheless, traditional practices permit institutions to make claims for the distinctiveness of their environment, their faculty, and their degree. What happens to the totality of the educational experience when some of these variables change? What is the new role of faculty in non-traditional studies? How can we assess the quality of student growth and development?

The questions are many; the answers are few. Chapter One sets the stage for thinking about new flexibilities within a conceptual framework of education as it is practiced. Following this overview, Chapters Two through Four will speak to more specific questions raised by recent worldwide interest in non-traditional alternatives. (Editors)

The phrase "non-traditional study" in higher education includes a vast array of educational programs. Basically, it refers to learning experiences that do not take place under the auspices and supervision of some formally recognized higher educational institution; or it may refer to learning that does take place under such auspices and supervision but differs significantly from the other formal educational efforts taking place there.* By this definition, correspondence instruction, which has been available in this country for years, would be regarded as a form of "non-traditional study." In addition, students who are regularly enrolled in a college or university but who take one or more courses under "independent study" arrangements (whereby they are not required to attend formal

* An alternative definition used in some Commission subcommittees is that non-traditional study consists of a set of learning experiences free of time and space limitations, organized so that the student may acquire new skills or attainments extending his personal, intellectual, esthetic, or vocational development. (Editors)

classes or to meet regularly with an instructor) would also be participating in a form of what we are here calling "non-traditional study."

Some of these educational programs (for example, continuing education or adult education programs) may not be designed to lead to any particular "credit" or recognition. Although important educational experiences are offered by these programs, they will not be a major focus here, since we are concerned primarily with educational experiences for which some form of summative evaluation or recognition is desired. In some cases we will be considering innovative instructional programs (that is, the educational *process*); in other cases the focus will be on the certification procedure (the educational *outcomes*). Both of these activities—new forms of teaching and new forms of certifying—are regarded in this paper as nontraditional educational programs to the extent that they are based on flexibility and an awareness of individual differences.

NEED FOR NON-TRADITIONAL PROGRAMS

Writing about the ills of formal education, particularly as it exists in this country, Ivan Illich (1971) argues that there is a fundamental difference between genuine education (learning that is primarily self-directed and continual) and "schooling" (a system of certification and classification, imposed on students by some external authority and directed at increasing material progress). "For most men," Illich contends, "the right to learn is curtailed by the obligation to attend school."

It is certainly not true that learning requires schools or other educational institutions as we think of them today; for, as Bruner (1966) has pointed out, "Learning is so deeply ingrained in man that it is almost involuntary" (p. 113). Nothing about the educational enterprise would deny this point of view, but certainly most American educators would argue that formal educational institutions serve as facilitators of the accumulation of knowledge and other basic skills and behaviors for most people who pass through the educational system. Such a position may or may not be correct; but, in the case of non-traditional study, it is not that important, either. The important point is that formal educational institutions are not necessary as learning contexts for *some* people (how many no one can say with assurance); and it therefore follows that these institutions should not be regarded as the only avenues to gaining recognition for educational growth and development. Formal educational institutions were designed to be appropriate for large groups of people. In higher education, institutions have employed the credit-per-course system, the large lectures, the prescribed syllabus, the frequent deadlines for assignments and evaluation, and all the rest, largely out of this need to deal with large numbers of students. Such an approach is therefore understandable; and for many, many students, in fact, it may be the optimal educational procedure. At the same time, it obviously cannot provide educational experiences based on the developmental needs of the individual student. All students—regardless of their educational backgrounds, personal dispositions, employment situations, family responsibilities, and the like—must generally find ways to deal with an educational system which was designed for the "average student."

Those responsible for college and university programs probably think that this mass-oriented form of education is the only feasible approach for one or both of two basic reasons: because they are convinced of the soundness of its educational premise (that most people, regardless of personal characteristics, tend to learn in the same ways) or because, given the great numbers of students, they can see no viable alternative to the current system. Both of these stances are based on inflexible outlooks. The first is inflexible in that it espouses a very narrow view of the learning process and the importance of the interaction between personal characteristics and learning experiences. The second view is inflexible in that it is unwilling to test the claim that any other pedagogical procedure would be more costly and cumbersome. It may well be that other, less traditional forms of education are *less* expensive, more efficient, and would result in a greater social contribution.*

PEOPLE HANDICAPPED BY TRADITIONAL EDUCATION

Much of the preceding argument or defense of the need for non-traditional study programs is based on the inflexible nature of the higher educational system—particularly its inability to respond to the needs of students who do not fit the mold. There are many different groups of people, with a host of personal orientations, who would seem to benefit greatly from more flexible or non-traditional forms of education. Such groups are considered in some detail in Chapter Two, but the need for variety and flexibility in providing learning experiences for diverse groups of people may be briefly illustrated by three examples of persons who are handicapped by traditional models of higher education.

* Of course, whether non-traditional study is more or less expensive than "regular" forms depends on the nature of the non-traditional program in question. It is generally true that educational costs increase with the frequency of faculty-student contact. Thus, certain kinds of "independent study" programs, for example, can be very expensive, as many college deans will attest. Still, many legislators are betting on the non-traditional programs to yield the same or more social good for much less money, a factor which no doubt explains the enthusiasm for non-traditional programs in some states. Until or unless they are proved wrong, many politicians and some educators will continue to support non-traditional educational programs, primarily because they are convinced that such programs are cheaper.

17

Non-Traditional Study: An Overview

Creative People. Certainly one can point to some institutions, or to departments within institutions, that have been responsive to the needs of creative students and have sensibly and flexibly met the needs of these students. By and large, however, higher education as it now exists has not provided a satisfactory educational experience for this type of unusual student. Heist (1968) has referred to creative college students as "transients," pointing out that college students identified as creative tend to have very high transfer or attrition rates. According to Heist, many creative students find their on-campus experiences "a pretty confining grind" or a "deadly routine," often void of novelty, challenge, or esthetic stimulation. Some of these students apparently beat the mundane routine by various noncurricular involvements, but often at a cost to their course work and grade records.

Elsewhere, Heist and Wilson (1968) argue that the educational experiences of the creative student must be based on "a degree of freedom which permits the creative student to opt for certain activities or experiences—such as special courses, unusual combinations of courses, or digressive reading ventures—which may be entirely unique to his immediate or future needs." Innovative, flexible, educational experiences clearly are necessary for such students. Flexibility, in fact, may be the most important ingredient. Such flexibility—designed to meet the needs of the creative student or any other non-traditional student—does not mean "lower standards" or "academic license." What it does or should mean is greater responsibility for the student to decide upon a learning style and pace more suitable to his own needs and dispositions, so that he is not hemmed in by the protocol of the traditional system.

Military Personnel. There is almost certainly no occupational group in this country as mobile as career military personnel. Each year, thousands upon thousands of military men and women, many of them attempting to earn college degrees through part-time educational programs of one kind or another, are transferred to another community. For such people, satisfactory fulfillment of the degree requirements at any one institution—especially considering the large number of academic credits "lost" in the transfer process and the typical one-year residence requirements of most institutions—is extremely difficult.

As one example, let us consider Sergeant X, a mythical (but very real, too) non-traditional student whose plight has been described by Furniss (1971). Sergeant X, a career military man, plans to retire after twenty years. When he does, he would like to have a college degree so that he can move from the army to a civilian job of some responsibility with no unnecessary delays. Now in his fifth year of service, he has time to study and attend classes, provided they are held in off-duty hours nearby. Realistically, however, he must expect to be on at least five different posts—two of them outside of the United States—before his retirement. Careful analysis of the educational prospects of Sergeant X makes it clear that the likelihood of his obtaining a college degree under the current system is slim indeed. In spite of the availability of correspondence courses offered by the armed forces, extension courses from various institutions, the College-Level Examination Program (CLEP), and all the rest—in spite of these, Sergeant X will be faced with numerous serious obstacles in his quest for a college degree.

He will find, first of all, that there is a great deal of curricular diversity from one institution to another, such that the major field course requirements at one institution will almost certainly be different from those at another. Furthermore, he will discover that there are no common quality standards across institutions. Academic achievement awarded six hours of credit at one institution—whether by performance on a CLEP exam, completion of courses on campus, or whatever —may earn him only three credits at another college and no credits at still another. Finally, of course, there is the problem of the residence requirement. Regardless of how much Sergeant X may know in his chosen major field, he will discover that unless he learns "one year's worth" of knowledge at one particular institution, that institution will not award him a degree with its name.

Mothers of School-Age Children. According to Kreps (1971), "In the search for models which typify the educational conditions, needs, and probable programs for various groups of nontypical college students, the middle-aged mother of school-age children is perhaps the most glaring example of unmet need and underutilized talent" (p. 1). Largely because higher education and subsequent professional employment were traditionally regarded as something for men only, a substantial number of women discontinued their formal education (often so that their husbands could continue theirs). Many of these women would now like to continue their formal education but find that the constraints are too numerous to make the effort worthwhile. Basically, their problems are much like those of Sergeant X: the difficulty of transferring previous learning experiences; the fact that they are often limited to instruction offered within commuting distances, since they must live at home; the often rigid regulations regarding certain course requirements, such as language, mathematics, and science; and so on.

The creative college student, the career military man, and the mother of school-age children are just three of many such case studies that could be cited as evidence for the need of greater flexibility in higher education. For these people and others who are "different," the concept of education as something which occurs within the confines of a campus Monday through Friday, broken up into little bits and pieces called "courses," usually "taught" via lectures—for these people such a concept of education is useless. (For that matter, such an educational procedure may not be the best one for *any* students, but that is not for us to decide here.)

"LOOSENING UP" THE TRADITIONAL SYSTEM

What are some examples of the kinds of activities that would "loosen up" the system for the non-traditional students just described? We have spoken of innovative instructional programs and flexible procedures for recognizing diverse forms of education; but what, in more specific terms, would make up some of the basic elements of these non-traditional undertakings?

Recognizing Benefits of Nonschool Experiences. As suggested earlier, education and learning occur in a wide variety of contexts and circumstances; and it is naïve indeed to deny the educational benefits of various experiences that take place outside the formal structure of our educational institutions. The number and variety of these experiences are almost infinite. For example, many Peace Corps volunteers, through their experiences in foreign countries, certainly could have accumulated valuable educational experiences. Why does the "regular" student obtain "credit" for a course in, say, student teaching while the Peace Corps student, who has taught for several years in a foreign school, receives no "credit" for his experiences? Why does a traditionally enrolled student earn credit for a course in something like "urban problems" while the VISTA worker, who has spent months in the ghetto working with those who live there, receives no such recognition? Clearly, some procedure must be provided for these kinds of genuine educational experiences to be recognized.

What is being urged here is recognition of *educational* experiences, not just experience. We are inclined to believe that educational credentials should not be assigned to various work or travel experiences unless academically relevant outcomes of those experiences can be demonstrated. Non-traditional study should not be regarded as a means of getting credit for having lived a "well-rounded" life. Rather, it should be a flexible program of granting recognition for academic accomplishment. "Granted the fact that merely to stay alive is highly educational, a distinction has to be made at some point between what people ordinarily do from day to day and what they should do if they are members of a college student body. There are many things that are beneficial to personal development—marriage, raising children, running a rock band—but not necessarily as part of the college curriculum" (Taylor, 1971, p. 92).

What we are suggesting, of course, is that there *are* many very important educational experiences to be had outside the formal college campus. Certain work experiences can be exceedingly relevant educationally; travel and reading on one's own can obviously be likewise; various kinds of leisure-time activities—attending concerts, visiting art galleries—are surely as educationally beneficial as certain "courses" in art appreciation. The list could go on and on. In fact, as Taylor again suggests, "to break out of the pattern of sixteen years of class-going is, in itself, a step ahead" (p. 93).

Facilitating Transfer of Credits. One of the greatest difficulties confronted by non-traditional students is that of transferring to a different institution. For many people (for instance, the mother of school-age children who wants to resume her education at the age of 35) the problem is confounded by a time lapse of many years; but even when the transfer is rather direct or occurs within one or two years of one's most recent educational matriculation, the transfer process can be a devastating experience. Almost without exception, the transfer student finds that the perceived value of his academic record depreciates significantly each time he moves from one institution to another. Even such general survey courses as "Introduction to Psychology," worth three academic credits at institution X, may not be accepted at institution Y, usually for vague reasons having to do with a perceived difference in the nature of the two courses.

Some of the loss-of-credit experiences are reasonable and understandable. Institutions do vary considerably in their academic programs, and the fact that a course title is the same on two different campuses does not ensure that the same subject-matter material is included or that the same competencies are called for. In fact, if institutions are serious about their claims to offer distinctive undergradute liberal-arts programs of one kind or another, it would be contradictory of them to accept without question the academic performances that students recorded at other institutions. Most of the decisions about the transfer process, however, are not wed so neatly to a clear educational philosophy. (How often, in fact, are such decisions made by an educational policies committee of the faculty, and how often by a clerk in the registrar's office?) The decisions about the transfer student's record—almost always operating to his loss rather than gain—are often based on whim or guesswork.

One possible means of diminishing the erosion of the academic credentials of transfer students would be to establish a national (or regional) credit bank or center, which might serve as a sort of clearinghouse for transfer students. Such a center might serve in an advisory capacity for the institutions to which students are submitting transcripts, assisting these institutions in making an objective and fair evaluation of the student's previous academic record. Conceivably, this center might also be empowered to grant its own degree. This latter function would probably not be a major activity of the credit bank, but might occur when a student is compelled to transfer frequently (such as our Sergeant X) and thus might accumulate a large number of academic credits from various institutions, none of which could be persuaded to grant him their degree for one reason or another.

Non-Traditional Study: An Overview

Any suggestion for ways of facilitating the transfer of credits is scoffed at by certain critics of higher education simply because it nurtures what in their opinion is one of the worst features of American higher education—the credit system. Such critics argue that the accumulation of credits has become an end in itself. To the extent that this criticism is true it is a serious indictment.

At the same time, some means of quantifying one's knowledge or educational experiences is necessary and probably desirable. If one claims to "know psychology," it is surely not unreasonable to ask "How *much* psychology?" Or if one offers as evidence of his adequate preparation for an accountant's job the fact that he has "studied accounting," it hardly seems unjustified to inquire about the extent of his studies in that particular field. The credit system, as it currently exists in most institutions, is simply a means of recording the quantity (but not the quality) of these formal educational experiences. Some means of keeping track of the quantity aspect of education is appropriate, and blaming many or most of the problems of American higher education on the credit system hardly seems realistic.

Granting Credit by Examination. For the past twenty-five years, students who were not high school graduates could earn their secondary school diploma by passing an examination —the tests of General Educational Development (GED), administered by the American Council on Education. In view of the popularity and wide acceptance of the GED tests (by students and by employers and college admissions officers), it is somewhat surprising that similar avenues have not been open to those aspiring to the college degree. Outside of one or two locally administered credit-by-examination programs (such as the New York State College Proficiency Examination Program) and one nationally oriented program with credit decisions vested in the colleges (the College-Level Examination

Program of the College Entrance Examination Board), there is no nationally recognized procedure by which students may attempt to demonstrate that they know more than their academic credentials indicate.

The idea of earning college credit or even a college degree by examination is not new to certain other countries. In England, for example, a college degree has for many years been available by means of examination performance through the University of London.

The logic of a credit- or degree-by-examination program is straightforward: degrees ought to be awarded on the basis of what or how much one knows rather than how many credits he has accumulated. The counterargument is usually that achievement examinations tap only one of the many kinds of outcomes of an on-campus collegiate experience, and to award degrees on the basis of examination performance alone would distort or reduce the overall meaning of the college degree. Until sound evidence can be provided in support of the "other-outcomes" argument, however, there appears no good reason for not making these opportunities available to more students on a national basis.

Establishing Community-Based Educational Centers. In making the previous suggestions for changes in practices and policies, we have continued to view major educational programs as available through the current higher-education model; that is, through colleges and universities that exist as separate institutions, independent from the community in which they happen to be located. Princeton University, for example, does not *need* to be located in Princeton, New Jersey. The educational programs of the vast majority of higher-education institutions are not an integral part of the community in which they are located. The fact that some members of the community can and do avail themselves of certain benefits of the institution's presence (via lectures, concerts, athletic events, and the

25

like) in no way suggests that the town-gown relationship is a mutually dependent one. The major activities of these institutions are generally conducted with a rather detached view of the needs of the surrounding community.

A new model for higher education that would be particularly appropriate for the non-traditional student is the community-based college or university. In this new model, the community would form an integral part of the institution or, in effect, would become the institution. The public library, for example, would serve as the major educational center or base for the learning experiences of the college's clientele. Various people with demonstrated skills and competencies in the community (local professional people, accomplished artists and musicians, craftsmen of various types—people who do not necessarily possess the credentials often required of "regular" faculty members) would form the faculty of the community-based institution. The "curriculum" would be diverse, and "courses" would probably consist of various experiences and readings that do not fit neatly into the current curricular packages of sociology, psychology, and the like, as we currently think of them.

The student body would literally be anyone in the community with an interest in learning, and all resources in the community—facilities, people, programs—would be drawn upon in the learning process. Naturally, not all higher educational institutions would easily fit this model or should attempt to modify their programs so that they would. But many existing institutions could easily go this route, and it would be most appropriate for them to do so. These universities without walls would be filling a great need in American higher education.

Establishing Counseling and Information Centers. Kreps (1971) describes the biggest problem of Mrs. Smith, a 35-year-old mother of three school-age children who wants to return to college, as follows: ". . . the major stumbling block

26

to Mrs. Smith's education is one that surfaces before she even resumes the process. She has no *counseling* appropriate to her needs and aspirations; no one in the education establishment, moreover, is offering any particular encouragement to her" (p. 4). Unquestionably, any move toward expanded opportunities for higher education would require a full-scale, high-quality program of educational guidance and information. Flexible, non-traditional opportunities can assist only those who know about them and who have accurate perceptions of the way the diverse programs fit their personal needs, backgrounds, and current conditions. What seems to be needed is a network of guidance and information centers where potential students can learn about the variety of programs and opportunities available to them. The major requirement for these centers would be the collection and dissemination of accurate information. Other activities (such as certain kinds of educational testing and counseling) might naturally follow; but, at least at the outset, the primary focus should be on providing information—the information, for instance, that students can pick up a high school equivalency certificate through satisfactory test performance; that not all correspondence schools are profit-making ruses; that in some states students can earn a college degree via examination. Just by making people aware that such possibilities exist, these centers would be performing a creditable service.

DIFFICULTIES AND ISSUES IN NON-TRADITIONAL STUDY

None of the foregoing arguments *for* flexible, non-traditional study programs should ignore the very real difficulties and limitations that must be worked out before such programs can be successful. Some of these problems are problems of mechanics (for instance, how to evaluate student performance); others are far more philosophical in nature. In this section we consider just a few of these problems.

Emphasizing Degrees Rather Than Learning. Though the non-traditional study "movement" is giving attention to both the educational process and the means of certification, it is often more concerned with certification. The underlying rationale for this approach is simply that we should be more concerned about what people know and what skills they possess, and less concerned about how they gained their knowledge or learned their skills.

These programs are virtually certain to be criticized (in some cases have already been criticized) for encouraging degree-getting behavior and implicitly attaching more value to the degrees than the education. This criticism may well be true, though it is doubtful that we will ever know. In any event, the criticism can also be made of traditional forms of higher education. The economic benefits associated with the attainment of a college degree in this country, in fact, operate as a reinforcement of obtaining degrees, not necessarily becoming well educated. Two persons with the same general knowledge and skills in a certain field—one who obtained his knowledge "on his own" and one who did so via a formal college or university program—are treated differently by employers. The one who received college credit for his studies will now receive credit of another kind in the form of a better job and higher income than his self-educated counterpart. Clearly, being educated is not sufficient for certain kinds of job entry and promotion, whereas a *certified* education may be.

It is even true that "certified education" offers no great economic advantages unless it is of sufficient *quantity.* (Quality of education does appear to make some difference but not nearly so much as quantity.) (See Levin et al., 1971; Witmer, 1970.) Of two persons who attended X college—one with extremely high grades but who withdrew ten credit hours shy of the total required for graduation, and the other with middling grades who accumulated the prescribed number of credits to graduate—the graduate would almost certainly be rewarded (in terms of job entry and salary) more than the nongraduate.

In any event, it is doubtlessly true that obtaining the degree or certificate has become all-important in American higher education. Whether this is the fault of the educators or the employers who hire their students is not a question to be addressed here. The point is—degrees count; and it makes no sense to withhold this certification from those of high educational attainment whose backgrounds do not include a prescribed number of experiences within the formal educational academy on the unsubstantiated (and perhaps irrelevant) grounds that those opting for a non-traditional program are less interested (than those in traditional programs) in learning for learning's sake.

Maintaining Quality. Some of those reluctant to endorse the concept of non-traditional study are concerned primarily with the problem of maintaining quality, or preventing a deterioration in "what the degree stands for." Though there are numerous ambiguities and uncertainties in that statement, it is at the same time fairly easy to point to a number of experiences and "quality-control" steps that are characteristic of the traditional college program. Graduates of traditional institutions, for example, generally sit through at least thirty different courses with their attendant requirements, deadlines, and esoteric features. In so doing they are sometimes interacting with acknowledged scholars in their fields—an experience which usually cannot be claimed by those who do not attend a "regular" college. In addition, students at traditional institutions are evaluated, at various steps along the way, by these same experts and scholars—people who are presumably decent judges of competence in those they have taught. (Whether they in fact are is a question that has been debated for years in the academy, and one which cannot be discussed in detail here.) This step-wise evaluation process, many argue, is a built-in quality-control mechanism that assures certain standards and competencies in those who graduate from traditional college programs—a sort of guarantee that cannot be claimed for non-traditional programs.

Though there is an appealing logic to the quality-control argument—and it should not be lightly dismissed—there is a major flaw. The great diversity which characterizes higher education has resulted in a system in which the range of skills, knowledge, and other behaviors required for acceptable evaluations at each step along the path toward the degree is extremely large. Course performance resulting in an "A" grade at one institution would result in failure at certain other colleges. Because of this great difference across institutions—a diversity we have always cherished—it is simply foolish to argue that a traditional college degree has uniform meaning or connotes some minimal educational standards.

This leads to the inevitable question: What is a college degree *supposed* to mean? There is probably no one answer; instead, each college can make separate claims for the meaning of *its* degree. With the meaning of degrees viewed in this way, there is nothing to prohibit the non-traditional degree from simply specifying the characteristics it presumes to ensure among its graduates and letting it go at that.

Related closely to the general problem of maintaining quality is the more specific difficulty of recruiting and holding a competent faculty. This task, an extremely difficult one even in the more traditional institutions, will be particularly vexing for non-traditional programs. For one thing, there is the matter of institutional reputation and prestige. Even the traditional colleges which are not well known and highly regarded academically have difficulties in attracting first-rate faculty members. Naturally the best people are inclined to look for positions where there are other recognized scholars, excellent facilities, opportunities for visibility, and the like. Non-traditional programs not only lack reputations but, worse, they are different. The prospective faculty members cannot always be sure quite what to expect in terms of the nature of the courses to be taught, the procedures to use in teaching those courses, and the people who will be the students. If he or she finds that the experience is not quite what was expected or hoped for, then there is the problem of gaining entry (or returning) to one of the traditional faculties with a non-traditional *vita*.

From the point of view of those responsible for the non-traditional program, faculty recruitment and evaluation will be extremely difficult, even more so than is the case with traditional institutions. Presumably, there will be little or no interest in rewarding research productivity, and quality of teaching will be the primary characteristic to be evaluated. To further complicate the already difficult task of evaluating teaching, what teaching means will have to undergo careful rethinking. In many non-traditional programs the nature of the student-teacher relationship will be considerably different from what most faculty members have experienced. When viewed in the context of the need to establish credibility and ensure a high quality program, the recruitment of an able faculty may turn out to be one of the most difficult hurdles facing those who attempt to establish non-traditional programs.

Evaluation. The evaluation of traditional educational programs and students in them has for years been giving educators headaches. Non-traditional programs have all of the problems of evaluation in the more typical settings, plus a whole set of difficulties all their own. First of all, evaluation in non-traditional settings has a somewhat different purpose. While the usual goals of evaluation in education—improvement of the educational program, clarification of the purposes of the curriculum—apply, one other purpose seems to loom extremely important in the evaluation of non-traditional programs—namely, establishing *credibility*. In the first years of non-traditional programs especially, it will be essential to convince others who might be wary—other educators, employers, potential students, the public—that flexible, non-traditional programs can still be rigorous and demanding, resulting in graduates of quality.

Essentially, there are two problems of evaluation here. The first has to do with the assessment of individual student growth and development (the readiness of individual students to receive the degree, to proceed to more advanced courses or reading lists, and the like). The second problem of evaluation has to do with the quality and effectiveness of the non-traditional program (whether student growth and competence at the time of graduation is comparable to that of students who graduate from more traditional institutions; whether the efficiency of such programs—in monetary costs, time involved, and the like—is comparable; and so on). These two kinds of evaluation are closely related, of course; and both are necessary for the establishment of the credibility we spoke of earlier.

The problem is an immense one, however; for the notions of program efficiency and individual student quality, in certain respects, can be expected to be at odds with each other. For example, one of the simplest ways to ensure individual student quality—and hence build a broad credibility base—is to set extremely high standards that must be met before students can be awarded a non-traditional degree. The University of London has done just that. Students aspiring to the University of London external degree must meet standards *at least* as high as those that exist for internal students. This has resulted, however, in an extremely high attrition rate. Obviously, given students of equal ability, standards can be expected to be inversely related to percentage of entrants completing the degree. But if the standards are so high that only

Rodney T. Hartnett

10 per cent of the students graduate, the efficiency of the program will be quite low (or the cost per graduate will be quite high).* This same problem must be faced by the British Open University. Supported by some because of great expectations of economy, this university may have an attrition rate of 80 per cent or higher, at least during its first few years (Maclure, 1971). Clearly, some means must be found for maintaining standards which establish credibility for the degree but are not so stringent as to cause an unreasonably high attrition rate.

Whatever the nature of the evaluation task, it is quite likely that the evaluation will rely, to some extent, on student performance on standardized achievement examinations in the various subject-matter fields. In fact, in those non-traditional programs where there is no instructional component and the major thrust of the effort is on certification, student performance on such standardized tests might reasonably be expected to be the most important criterion for student evaluation. Even when the programs do include an instructional component and emphasize innovative educational experiences rather than certification, it is important to demonstrate that graduates of these programs know as much on standardized achievement measures as students who graduate from more conventional programs.

However, the use of standardized achievement measures in the evaluation of non-traditional programs and students has certain limitations. In programs that focus on educational certification, achievement measures designed to be

* Many proponents of non-traditional programs have compared the estimated cost per student with the same index at traditional institutions, in which case the non-traditional institutions fare quite well. However, since approximately 50 per cent of the entering students at a traditional institution graduate in four or five years, a comparison of costs *per graduate* might result in less encouraging data for the non-traditional programs.

broadly applicable (that is, appropriate to the learning experiences of a large group of people and, therefore, based on general principles and concepts of a field) may at the same time be highly correlated with measures of general intelligence. That this correlation is almost certain to occur highlights, of course, the conceptual difficulty that psychologists and educators have faced for years in attempting to distinguish between "achievement" and "aptitude." Many experts now feel that this distinction is artificial. They reject the notion that "aptitude" is a measure of "innate" talents and "achievement" a measure of learned talents and argue that both should be regarded as measures of knowledge in a given subject or skill at a specific point in time.

To the extent that the measures used for student evaluation in this context are comprised of the "g" factor (reflecting the *general* nature of cognitive skills required on such tests, a quality some regard as being synonymous with intelligence) it may well be that certification would be awarded to those students who are simply bright, without regard for other indicators of accomplishment which are generally regarded as important in earning a college degree. For programs concerned primarily with certification, this would likely mean that only highly intelligent people would be the likely beneficiaries of the non-traditional procedure. This, in itself, is not an indictment. But it *is* a limitation of the scope of the non-traditional certification programs, and it must be recognized and considered—especially before a great deal is attributed to the programs' potential for highly motivated but not-so-intelligent aspirants.

For non-traditional programs that include an instructional component and therefore can anchor the student evaluations to a specific curriculum or schedule of academic experiences, the fuzziness of the aptitude-achievement distinction might be less of a problem. In this case the achievement measures could (and should) be built upon the specific objectives and features of the academic program offered at each institution. Thus, the achievement measure could be rather specialized and less typified by the generality and broad principles characteristic of the tests that would probably be employed in the programs focusing solely on certification. Here one confronts another danger, however; namely, that the achievement measures (although originally developed on the basis of the already-decided-upon learning experiences) might begin to dictate the curriculum or educational program of the students. Furthermore, if a program of educational experiences is to be developed in accordance with the backgrounds, needs, and characteristics of individual students—implying that each student, regardless of his "major," may pursue a study program unlike that of any other— then the appropriateness of any one measure of achievement is certainly questionable. Here one might argue that while different approaches to learning should be encouraged, the basic purposes and educational goals should remain the same—so that the achievement measures will be appropriate. Clearly, such difficulties cannot be solved satisfactorily unless early attention is given to the question of the goals of the specific non-traditional study programs.

Even aside from the difficulties of using standardized achievement measures in non-traditional programs, it makes sense to employ more than one criterion in evaluation of both the non-traditional program and the non-traditional student. As Webb and his colleagues (1969) have pointed out, single classes of measurement are bound to include error. However, when empirical findings are confirmed by two or three independent measurement processes, the likelihood of error is considerably reduced. "If a proposition can survive the onslaught of a series of imperfect measures, with all their irrelevant error, confidence should be placed in it" (p. 3). The trick, of course, is to make sure that whatever error *is* contained in the different measures comes from a different source. In the present con-

35

text, achievement tests may contain considerable item-sampling error, "error" in the choice of items that make up the test. Therefore, any supplemental measure chosen should be one that is free of item-sampling error; such a measure would be faculty ratings. This measure does include a form of error not contained in the standardized tests—errors that might stem from a rater's poor judgment; his lack of acquaintance with the trait in question; his tendency unduly to allow a single characteristic of the ratee, good or bad, to influence his impression of the other characteristics in question (usually called the *halo effect*); and the like. But, used together, these two criteria—standardized tests and faculty ratings—might complement each other and dovetail well as measures of program and student accomplishment. Other criteria for certification of student accomplishments might include students' self-ratings, expert evaluations of various student products and projects, and (for programs such as VISTA or the Peace Corps) supervisory ratings.

Finally, those who are attempting to evaluate non-traditional programs might consider the techniques employed by accrediting associations. Though not dismissing student characteristics altogether, such an approach places more emphasis on *program* characteristics. Thus, teams of experts might visit the center or centers in which non-traditional programs are offered, talking with the staff members, reviewing the materials that describe the programs, assessing the quality of available facilities and services (library, programmed learning materials, and the like), and evaluating the textbooks (or other sources) used in the courses offered.

NEED FOR FLEXIBILITY

We shall argue here that greater flexibility—in awarding recognition for various academic experiences and in struc-

Rodney T. Hartnett

turing the educational process itself—is vitally necessary to higher education in this country. Essentially, this greater flexibility would be an expression of awareness that learning can and does take place in different ways for different people and that to continue to provide only one form of instruction and recognition is to be wasteful of the country's richest resources.

This is not intended to imply that many institutions of higher education are not now performing excellent educational functions. "Traditional" is not meant to be pejorative, any more than "non-traditional" is necessarily positive. The point is that there should be both. Students should have options, at least far more than are now available. For years American higher education has prided itself on its diversity, claiming to have a wide variety of postsecondary educational programs available to students with heterogeneous backgrounds, abilities, and interests. Much of the so-called diversity, however, has been more imaginary than real, at least in any important sense. For too long too many students have *not* had meaningful choices available to them. As stated in the report of the College Entrance Examination Board's Commission on Tests (1970, p. 39): "People are . . . diverse, more so than colleges have yet learned to take into account in their procedures, their programs, or their instruction. Colleges must change in this respect if everyone is to go to college."

It is questionable, of course, that everyone *should* go to college. Nevertheless, American higher education has not been responsive to the wide array of backgrounds, interests, and current living situations of students who *are* interested in postsecondary education and who have the ability and motivation to benefit from college if realistic opportunities were available. For these potential students the unnecessary barriers to a college education must be eliminated.

REFERENCES

BRUNER, J. S. *Toward a Theory of Instruction.* Cambridge, Mass.: Harvard University Press, 1966.

College Entrance Examination Board. *Report of the Commission on Tests.* Vol. I. *Righting the Balance.* New York: College Board, 1970.

FELDMAN, K., AND NEWCOMB, T. *The Impact of College on Students.* San Francisco: Jossey-Bass, 1969.

FURNISS, W. T. *Degrees for Nontraditional Students: An Approach to New Models,* A.C.E. Special Report. Washington, D.C.: American Council on Education, April 9, 1971.

HEIST, P. "Creative Students: College Transients." In Paul Heist (Ed.), *The Creative College Student: An Unmet Challenge.* San Francisco: Jossey-Bass, 1968.

HEIST, P., AND WILSON, R. "Curricular Experiences for the Creative." In Paul Heist (Ed.), *The Creative College Student: An Unmet Challenge.* San Francisco: Jossey-Bass, 1968.

ILLICH, I. *Deschooling Society.* New York: Harper & Row, 1971.

KREPS, J. "Nontraditional Students: The Case of Mrs. Smith." Paper prepared for a meeting of the Commission on Academic Affairs, American Council on Education, Washington, D.C., May 16–17, 1971.

LEVIN, H. M., GUTHRIE, J. W., KLEINDORFER, G. B., AND STOUT, R. T. "School Achievement and Post-School Success: A Review," *Review of Educational Research,* 1971, *41*(1), 1–16.

MACLURE, S. "England's Open University: Revolution at Milton Keynes," *Change,* 1971, *3*(2), 62–68.

TAYLOR, H. *How to Change Colleges.* New York: Holt, 1971.

WEBB, E., CAMPBELL, D., SCHWARTZ, R., AND SECHREST, L. *Unobtrusive Measures: Nonreactive Research in the Social Sciences.* Chicago: Rand-McNally, 1969.

WITMER, D. R. "Economic Benefits of College Education," *Review of Educational Research,* 1970, *40*(4), 511–523.

2

K. Patricia Cross, J. Quentin Jones

Problems of
Access

Many thousands of individuals are eager for new
and continuing educational opportunities. Some students need
greater flexibility in scheduling—courses, counseling, and financial assistance designed for part-time learners. Other students, with few credentials but with rich backgrounds of experience, need greater flexibility in the definition and certification of
educational experience. Still others seek "portable" academic
credits that can move with them as they continue their learning in new communities. Others, with broad-ranging minds but

restricted physical mobility, await developments that will bring education to students instead of always vice versa.

A number of changes in the society have dictated the escalation of interest in education for people of all ages, but perhaps the greatest force has been the recognition that knowledge is power. For the individual, education is the pathway to a better job, a better salary, and more of the good things of life. For government, education provides the potential power for solving social problems such as poverty, unemployment, racism, and crime. For business, knowledge is the power to produce the ideas and the goods to feed the insatiable hunger of the American people for a rising standard of living. For society, education holds the hope of preparing citizens to accept personal responsibility for solving problems such as environmental pollution, drug usage, overpopulation, and racism.

Obviously, the American people—individually and collectively—have compelling reasons for supporting the concept of lifelong learning and freedom of access to it. Yet there are people who find it difficult, if not impossible, to join the educational mainstream. Chapter Two is about groups of potential learners who need new alternatives to traditional education. If there is to be full equality of educational opportunity, new options must be offered in instruction, counseling, and the recognition of educational achievement.(Editors)

Historically, American higher education has developed its programs primarily for young, single, unemployed adults who can devote their full time and attention to the four-year pursuit of a college education. These students, however, do *not* form the majority of the learning force in America. With considerable ingenuity, eager learners across the country have devised many opportunities for learning outside of recognized channels. By 1976 the number of people engaged in formal organized learning activities *outside* the recognized educational system will exceed the number of students in preschool, elementary, secondary, and higher education combined (Moses, 1970a). A study conducted by the National Opinion Research Center in 1961 concluded that more than half (56 per cent) of all adult studies involving formal attendance at classes, lectures, or discussion groups took place in churches, private businesses, YMCAs, government agencies, the armed forces, and community institutions other than schools or adult education centers (Johnstone and Rivera, 1965).

In a study by one of the nation's Educational Policy Research Centers, Moses (1970b) has analyzed the growth of America's "learning force" from 1940 to 1976. The figures in Table 1 illustrate the growth of the educational periphery compared with the educational core. The major criterion for inclusion in the "periphery" is that the activities occur outside traditional schools but involve participation in learning through an "organized structured learning situation." The "educational core" refers, of course, to activities taking place within schools and colleges traditionally regarded as educational institutions.

Moses (1970b) is highly critical of present tendencies to ignore the actual and potential educational contribution of the periphery. He points out that we will need to revise our thinking and priorities to include the periphery when considering public policy decisions affecting resource allocation. At present, information about participation in the periphery is not even collected by public information agencies. The result, of course, is that planning is unnecessarily restrictive and little attention is given to the integration of educational experiences provided by the core and the periphery. Planning, it would appear, should start with the needs of people rather than with institutions. This chapter is about people and their learning needs.

TABLE 1. THE LEARNING FORCE (1940–1976)
(millions)

	1940	1950	1955	1960	1965	1970	1976
						Current Estimates	
I. The Educational Core							
1. Pre-primary	.7	1.3	2.0	2.7	3.1	4.4	5.5
2. Elementary	20.5	21.0	26.0	29.1	32.0	32.3	30.0
3. Secondary	7.1	6.5	9.3	13.0	16.8	19.8	22.1
4. Undergraduate	1.4	2.4	2.4	3.2	4.9	6.5	8.3
5. Graduate	.1	.2	.2	.4	.6	.8	1.1
Subtotal	29.8	31.4	39.9	48.4	57.4	63.8	67.0
II. The Educational Periphery							
6. Organizational	8.2	10.2	10.9	13.0	14.5	21.7	27.4
7. Proprietary	2.5	3.5	3.5	4.0	7.8	9.6	18.1
8. Antipoverty	—	—	—	—	2.8	5.1	7.0
9. Correspondence	2.7	3.4	3.5	4.5	5.0	5.7	6.7
10. TV	—	—	—	.0	5.0	7.5	10.0
11. Other adult	3.9	4.8	5.1	6.8	9.1	10.7	13.2
Subtotal	17.3	21.9	23.0	28.3	44.2	60.3	82.4
III. The Learning Force (I + II)	47.1	53.3	62.9	76.7	101.0	124.1	149.4

Source: Moses, 1970(a)

K. Patricia Cross, J. Quentin Jones

BARRIERS TO TRADITIONAL EDUCATION

Three characteristics of traditional education pose
barriers to large numbers of people. First, the notion that learning requires physical presence in the classroom restricts access
for those with physical handicaps, those in geographically
remote areas, and those who are temporarily or permanently
confined—for example, prison inmates and mothers of small
children. Second, the concept that it is the accumulation of
credit hours that fulfills degree requirements handicaps those
whose lives dictate a mobility too great to collect sufficient
credits at a single degree-granting institution—servicemen,
business transfers, wives leaving college before the completion
of their own degrees. Finally, the idea that education is the
learner's major activity and that it customarily takes place
between 9 A.M. and 5 P.M. on working days creates scheduling
problems for vast numbers of potential part-time learners. In
a sense, these barriers bear little relationship to learning; they
can be said to be problems of being in the right place at the
right time. Some people lack mobility, some are too mobile,
and some have scheduling problems.

Geographical Barriers. Numerically, the largest group
of people denied access to postsecondary education because of
limitations related to their physical presence on campus are
those who are handicapped by geographical remoteness. In rural
areas, distance may be measured in miles and the lack of public transportation, but in many urban areas congestion makes
commuting to a college a time-consuming task that must
often compete with full-time jobs and family responsibilities.
Willingham (1970) concludes that less than half of the United
States populace live within a forty-five-minute commuting distance of a free-access (low-tuition, low-selectivity) college.
Stated numerically, more than one hundred million people can

43

be classified as geographically remote from traditional free-access educational opportunities. Accessibility varies enormously by region, but throughout the country the problems are most serious in rural areas and in the largest cities. According to Willingham, there is a serious deficiency of accessible institutions of higher education in twenty-three of the twenty-nine largest metropolitan areas of the country.

Commuting distance from educational opportunity is not the only deterrent to educational participation. The problem of the relative confinement of young mothers shows up again and again in studies of continuing learning. Stecklien and associates (1966) found that the typical student in Minnesota's TV College is the 31-year-old mother (with one child) seeking a bachelor's degree in teaching or the liberal arts. Johnstone and Rivera (1965) report that women are 22 per cent more likely than men to feel house-bound; among persons under 35, a substantially larger number of men than women are engaged in some form of study (33 per cent to 25 per cent) while older men and women enter the learning force at equal rates.

The physically handicapped and prison inmates have ample time for study and many have the desire to participate in substantial programs of education. Although more than 100,000 persons leave federal and state prisons each year, few of them receive the kind of training, while in prison, that enables them to compete successfully for jobs. Tragically, two thirds of the prison population are under 35 years of age, and most adult prisoners are school dropouts (Collins and Weisberg, 1966). Despite their poor educational records, the intelligence of prisoners is not much different from that of the general population.

Society is just beginning to recognize the very important role that education can play in the lives of people whose access to opportunity is inhibited by their inability to get to the campus, and yet very few institutions have attempted to take education to the student.

The examples of subgroups needing alternatives to on-campus study could be extended. The point is, however, that the conventional notion that certifiable learning takes place only in the classroom presents an educational handicap to literally thousands of people. Research is sparse and inadequate, but there is evidence that restriction of physical mobility is a major factor increasing the attraction of non-traditional educational alternatives (Hoban, 1965; Stecklien et al., 1966).

Barrier of "Accumulating Credits." Let us look now at the other extreme of the mobility handicap. Servicemen and women constitute a large group of potential students whose frequent moves interfere with the accumulation of degree credits. Their handicap is created by the notion that a single educational institution must be responsible for certifying that their learning adds up to a degree. The military services, however, represent a prime example of the kinds of non-traditional alternatives that can be offered to overcome or at least substantially reduce the handicap of excessive mobility as a barrier to full educational opportunity. Thousands of courses are provided by the military services and the United States Armed Forces Institute (USAFI). As a matter of fact, the armed forces are the nation's largest supplier of correspondence courses, accounting for 60 per cent of the total enrollment and serving 1.77 million people. In 1969, the worldwide enrollment in USAFI was 274,000, with 59 per cent enrolled in correspondence courses and 41 per cent in group-study classes (Sharon, 1971).

The great popularity of the educational services offered to military personnel must be partly attributed to the active role played by the Commission on the Accreditation of Service Experiences in seeking and recommending college credit for courses taken during active service. Nearly a million tests were administered by USAFI in 1969, and a recent survey of colleges and universities indicates that 73 per cent granted credit to veterans for formal service school programs or through credit by examination (Sharon, 1971). The military services have devised a varied and comprehensive educational program to help their excessively mobile population overcome the handicap introduced by traditional concepts of what constitutes a certifiable learning experience.

Not all young people are so fortunate. Young women who leave college and university communities upon the completion of their husbands' degrees are usually handicapped in obtaining full degree credit for work completed. Shelden and Hembrough (1964) report that more than half (57 per cent) of the married women students and students' wives who had entered the Urbana-Champaign community in the year prior to the study expected to leave the university area in two years or less—not enough time to add up to a University of Illinois degree, especially when part-time-student status is a necessity for most married women. And yet 71 per cent of the young women without a bachelor's degree expressed the desire to obtain one.

The number of people who experience difficulty in credentialing their knowledge is really quite large, and there is obvious interest in seeking a solution to the problem. In the six-month period from January through June of 1971, the College-Level Examination Program (CLEP) received over 146,000 requests for information about taking examinations for college credit. By June, the CLEP office was receiving 2,500 requests per week for information. This wave of interest was generated by a low-key advertising campaign simply informing people that a channel existed for converting knowledge to academic credits.

Among the many thousands of people who are experiencing difficulty with credentialing are those who study outside of official educational channels; those whose life circumstances prohibit their remaining in one place long enough for credits to add up to a degree; and those whose credits are "too old" to apply to a degree. The latter situation is especially common among older married women, who may have left college in their youth to marry or have families or because they moved from the community upon the completion of their husbands' degrees. Many of these women, ready to enter the labor market, would like to apply for jobs that offer a challenge to their intellectual abilities, but they are constantly thwarted by employers' stipulations of degree requirements.

Scheduling Barriers. Finally, let us look at examples of groups of people handicapped by the assumption that education is a full-time activity taking place largely between the hours of 9 A.M. to 5 P.M. on weekdays. Scheduling is a problem for almost anyone who wishes to combine educational activities with other adult responsibilities. Johnstone and Rivera (1965) report that the most common reasons for enrolling in adult study are job-related. Thus, it is not surprising that almost 75 per cent of all participants in adult study are in the labor force, and 62 per cent of them are employed full time. These figures represent huge numbers of people who have shown an obvious desire to pursue formal learning activities outside of what is considered "regular" class hours. But full-time employees are not the only members of the learning force to face scheduling problems.

Married women, with and without children, constitute another very large market for part-time study in "off" hours. For example, almost three fourths of the married women living near enough to the University of Illinois to participate in traditional educational offerings said that they could attend school only part time, and evening classes were twice as popular with the group as were regularly scheduled classes. One student confessed, "When I was single and a college undergraduate, I know that I took the privilege of attending college for granted; now I would give anything in the world to be able to go to school again. I can go only at night or on Saturdays" (Shelden and Hembrough, 1964, p. 49).

Financial Barriers. Scheduling is not the only problem faced by adults who cannot make formal education a full-time activity. Although, according to one survey of 750 colleges and universities (Oltman, 1970), 95 per cent "offer opportunities for mature women to complete degrees," Mattfeld (1971) points out that only 49 per cent of these made *any* concessions in rate of work, class hours, or customary academic policies or practices to fit the needs of mature women. Many institutions even have fee schedules wherein excessively high unit costs for part-time study close the door to thousands of potential students. Johnstone and Rivera (1965) report that the problem of finances (although most serious for younger adults with growing families) was mentioned more frequently than any other by adults of all ages who were classified as having high motivation for participation in part-time study.

Restricted Definitions of Education. One has only to read the popular press to know that there is widespread discontent with both the form and the content of traditional education. The most vocal of the critics are some highly able young people whose present rejection of traditional educational opportunities may pose problems for them as well as society now or later in their lives. To all appearances these young people have the opportunity to participate fully in the educational opportunities available, but the literature is replete with research describing their alienation from traditional programs of study.

Heist (1968) has identified a group of young people with high potential for intellectual creativity who have exceptionally high transfer or attrition rates from traditional colleges. The problem is likely to increase. Trow (1970, pp. 53–54) has described the involuntary attendance of "large numbers of students who really do not want to be in college, have not entered into willing contract with it, and do not accept the values or the legitimacy of the institution." Some of these students have defied societal expectations to found their own "free universities" as alternatives to the constraints of academic programs; others have simply dropped out.

At the other end of the spectrum from turned-off high-potential youth are turned-off young people who have had dismal school experiences in the past. Of all of the possible reasons for failing to continue education, a poor record of academic achievement looms largest (Cross, 1971). Poorly motivated and fearing further failure, these youth become increasingly alienated from the traditional academic curriculum of the educational core. The open door of the community colleges swings wide enough to admit them, but the programs that they find there are frequently similar to their experience with traditional education in the past; as a result, their stay on the campus is of brief duration. Improved access to traditional programs of education is unlikely to result in greater educational opportunity unless the programs offered are responsive to learners' needs.

The alienation of some of the radicals and the disadvantaged young from traditional educational establishments is broadly recognized. Less well recognized is the estrangement of many adults from formal instruction in the schools. Fewer than one adult in five, for example, would turn to regular schools or colleges to develop proficiency in a foreign language, even though this kind of instruction is in rather abundant supply in the schools (Johnstone and Rivera, 1965).

EDUCATIONAL NEEDS AND INTERESTS TODAY

All of the barriers discussed have the effect of limiting access to existing educational opportunities. Removal of such barriers is one way to improve access; but unless education offers what potential students want to learn, the removal of barriers will not result in improved access. What reasons do people have for wanting further education?

The reasons people give for pursuing formal learning vary with age, sex, socioeconomic status, past educational achievement, and a host of other variables that change as personal and social conditions change. Threats to the environment will propel some persons to seek new learning. Technological unemployment will necessitate formal study for others. The potential for new career opportunities will attract groups, such as ethnic minorities and women, whose education has failed to make much difference in the past. Rising educational requirements are facing employees in business and in government. Some employees seek educational credentials to compete with younger, better-educated employees; some need new learning to handle the increasing complexity of their jobs; some need certification to meet newly legislated educational requirements.

A national study of the learning interests of adults (Johnstone and Rivera, 1965) reveals no lack of interest in learning; 71 per cent of the adults surveyed expressed a desire to learn more about some particular area. Not all these adults, however, were considered by the researchers to be potential participants in formal courses of instruction, but Johnstone and Rivera conclude that nearly half of the adult population can be seriously regarded as potential students. Numerically, in their estimate, fifty million persons have *thought* about taking a course. The desire to learn is closely related to necessity and to past experience. Not surprisingly, young people recognize a greater need to learn new things than older people do (83 per cent of those in their twenties and 35 per cent of those in their 70s could think of something they would like to know more about); and college graduates are more likely to continue their interest in learning than grade school graduates (87 per cent to 50 per cent).

Likewise, the reasons for continued learning vary from group to group. Job-centered reasons are primary among younger people, whereas the goals of older adults are much less pragmatic and utilitarian. In 1961, when the study was conducted, men were more likely than women to express vocational motivations; today, however, education for job advancement may play an increasingly important role in the educational motivations of women. Socioeconomic status is also an important variable in educational motivation. Men and women from lower socioeconomic levels are much more likely to take courses to prepare for new jobs than to advance in present ones, whereas the opposite is true for those from higher socioeconomic levels.

There is no question that the need for education for vocational purposes is escalating rapidly. But talk of the four-day week and the increasing leisure of today's worker may make new educational opportunities for the use of leisure time even more imperative.

Learning for work and learning for leisure may play equally important roles in the decades ahead. The demands for lifelong learning opportunities are escalating rapidly. Johnstone and Rivera (1965) predict an adult education boom for the 1970s and 1980s that is comparable to the expansion of regular school enrollments in the 1950s and 1960s. Education seems to be one of those commodities that creates its own demand. The more education you have, the more you want. As the nation becomes better educated, the needs and desires of individuals and of the society will create untold demands for new and meaningful choices in education.

We must begin now to make realistic plans for increasing access to educational opportunity to meet the inevitable demand. The removal of existing barriers and the development of relevant new programs are two essential steps in making educational opportunity available to a broader segment of the population. The landmark study of adult education sponsored by the Carnegie Corporation (Johnstone and Rivera, 1965) has furnished a valuable start on the collection of information about the characteristics of the adult learning force. A systematic and continuing program of research and development will be necessary to guide the implementation of non-traditional studies. Particular attention should be given to the collection of information about the heretofore ignored educational periphery and the interface between the core and the periphery. The "adequacy" of existing opportunities can be judged, of course, only in relationship to the needs of people; and, as we have seen, needs and desires for particular kinds of learning opportunities vary enormously with the characteristics of the individual and the changes taking place in the broader society. Thus, research on needs and interests should be continuous to monitor a rapidly changing society; and it needs to take special cognizance of the differing educational needs of subgroups in the population.

COUNSELING: A TWO-WAY STREET

Theoretically at least, we could remove the barriers that inhibit access to existing educational opportunity and we could try to design programs that are relevant to the needs of people—and still not increase access to postsecondary education. People must be aware that opportunities exist, and we have a long way to go in providing new learners with adequate information. One adult in three has *no* knowledge of any place in his community where an adult can attend classes or receive instruction (Johnstone and Rivera, 1965). If our system of information *to* prospective students is inadequate, our channel for receiving information *from* students is even more in need of attention. Eighty per cent of a sample of adults enrolled in extension classes across the nation felt that they played *no part whatever* in determining what services would be available to them (Morton, 1953). A working two-way information network is needed to make the connections between learners and opportunities.

Although the term "counseling" has been used to describe the process of maximizing the fit between students and educational opportunities, counselors and guidance personnel have typically concentrated on informing students of available opportunities; they have rarely played an active role in adjusting the environment to the needs of students. Because the duality of the process is vital, we shall emphasize the point by using the concepts of "communications" and "flow of information" rather than the more traditional concept of counseling.

Communications to Students. Let us first look at the flow of information *to* the prospective student. How much do people know about the opportunities that are available? Some people know a lot; others know almost nothing. Two major elements that contribute to an individual's knowledge about educational opportunity are his own motivation and the actual availability of educational opportunities in his community. These two factors are by no means independent. The actual availability of educational facilities in the community increases awareness and heightens interest. The NORC study (Johnstone and Rivera, 1965) found, for example, that more than three quarters of the adults in cities known to contain numerous adult education facilities were aware of at least one resource. The relationship between availability and motivation also works the other way around. The influx of well-educated people into a community is quite likely to increase the educational offerings available by increasing the demand for such services.

It comes as no surprise that knowledge about educational opportunity varies directly with the amount of past education. Well-educated people are better informed than those with less education. Furthermore, people tend to know most about the educational offerings of institutions they are familiar with. For example, college-educated persons have more knowledge about courses offered by colleges, whereas high school graduates are more likely to be familiar with adult education courses offered under the auspices of the secondary schools. This research fact has implications for practice, since in any given community the concentration of offerings in colleges would attract students with some college education already. Unless care is taken in the counseling and information programs, the educational gap between the well educated and the less well educated in the community would increase simply because of past experience and familiarity with the source of instruction.

Socioeconomic status (SES), of course, also plays an important role in awareness of educational opportunity. When socioeconomic level and location (and therefore presumably availability) are combined, the differences in knowledge about educational opportunity are enormous. Johnstone and Rivera (1965) found that 85 per cent of those of high SES who lived in middle-sized communities knew about educational offerings, compared with only 19 per cent of low-SES respondents in small towns or rural areas. Consistent with the findings of Willingham (1970) regarding the lack of availability of free-access educational facilities in urban and rural areas, Johnstone and Rivera found that adults in middle-sized cities (50,000–2,000,000) were more likely to know about courses of instruction than those in either urban or rural areas.

Information about educational opportunity is dependent upon the interest of individuals. Persons who have thought about taking courses are more likely to know of at least one resource than those who would simply like to learn new things

—who, in turn, are better informed than those who are not interested in learning anything new at all. And finally, awareness of instructional facilities varies greatly with the subject matter. Most adults know where to go to learn to swim, dance, or type; few know where to go to learn auto mechanics, music appreciation, or speed reading.

Although research clearly demonstrates that knowledge about educational opportunity depends partly upon the characteristics of the individual and partly upon the availability of instruction, we need not accept these research findings as final. Intervention through programs of counseling and information can change things greatly. One good example of effective intervention is the educational counseling program of the armed forces.

Of all potential participants in continued learning, those in military service may have access to the best information system presently existing. Educational counseling of all personnel is required within thirty days of assignment to a military post and is available to all personnel thereafter on request. While the major thrust is made to encourage continuing education for those on active duty, those terminating their service also have access to information. Project Transition calls for the counseling of all personnel during the six months prior to separation. For those retiring from service, the Department of Defense Referral Program provides counseling about jobs and educational opportunities. While the quality of counseling and information naturally varies from post to post, the general philosophy of the military services has been to provide counseling and to encourage participation in educational activities.

Business, too, is playing an increasingly active role in encouraging employees to take advantage of educational opportunities. Drucker (1968, pp. 332–333) states the reality for business:

We need to punch big holes in the diploma curtain through which the able and ambitious can move even though they have not sat long enough on school benches to satisfy the schoolmasters' requirements. Employers, and especially large companies, need to look in their work force for the people of proven performance and willingness to achieve, though they lack the formal requirements. Indeed, to spend on this . . . money now spent on college recruitment would be highly profitable. With everyone trying to get the same college graduates, no one can hope to get anyone particularly outstanding or indeed anything but mediocrity. All one can do is bid up the entrance salary. Perhaps there are fewer big fish in the pond of those who have not gone to college. But the individual employer's chance of landing one of these big fish is infinitely greater in the pond where nobody else fishes than it is among college graduates, where he competes even for the minnows with every other employer in the land.

The role of business in continuing education for executives and management personnel has been well recognized, extending even to the construction of campuses and educational buildings by big corporations such as IBM, General Motors, General Electric, Mobil Oil, and Corning Glass. Less well known are the new programs of counseling, instruction, and credit by examination developed for hourly workers. The Ford Motor Company became one of the first in the United States to incorporate the College-Level Examination in its Continuing Education Program. The major thrust of the program is to identify talented people on the payroll and to expand their educational opportunities by means of granting degree credit by examination. Another example of the use by industry of the idea of college equivalency is the use of CLEP by the Packaging Corporation of America. While employee participation in CLEP is optional and at the discretion and interest of the employee, the corporation is willing to let satisfactory scores on the examinations stand in lieu of formal college attainment. Labor unions, too, have been active in encouraging education for the rank-and-file worker, and programs under the joint sponsorship of colleges and industry are beginning to flower along with tuition refunds and released time for educational activities.

Naturally, the employees who work in education-conscious businesses have opportunities and information not available to the nonaffiliated person. By the very nature of the enterprise, however, business and industry design their counseling and educational-opportunity programs for those on the payroll, with only minimal attention devoted to prospective employees.

Likewise, schools and colleges confine their services to students who are regularly enrolled or planning to enroll. It is the very rare and unusual counselor who is able and willing to help people seek non-traditional ways of learning. Some universities, especially land-grant institutions, have strong programs of extension services and some give a great deal of attention to the counseling of adults. The Minnesota Plan, established in 1960 at the University of Minnesota, is an outstanding example of a counseling program geared to the special needs of women who wish to return to school and to the labor market. The cornerstone of the Minnesota Plan is counseling, which means anything from talking over the fears and insecurity of returning to academic study to arranging for neighborhood seminars, wherein the university will send an instructor to the home if a group of sixteen or more are interested in a given subject. The plan also stands ready to assist with the practical problems of nursery care, financial aid, car pools, and job placement. Since a Carnegie grant sparked the development of the Minnesota Plan, numerous other universities have developed special centers to ease the transition for mature women from family responsibilities to continuing education.

Another example of a project aimed at the information needs of a particular group is the 150-page booklet sponsored by the Radcliffe Institute for Independent Study. The booklet, entitled *The Next Step* (White, 1964), seeks to inform women in the Greater Boston area of the opportunities available for education, volunteer work, or employment. Regular programs of study at the twenty-one colleges in the area, as well as the special adult education courses offered by core educational institutions, are described. Included also is information on summer programs, home study, and special programs offered by community centers, museums, hospitals, and proprietary schools. Readers are also referred to the Prospect Union Educational Exchange, a Boston clearinghouse for information on adult education courses that publishes an annual catalog listing more than 4,600 courses offered by two hundred approved schools for mature men and women.

Community colleges offer another alternative for serving the information needs of the public. The extremely rapid growth of community colleges has made them a strong contender for the role of community learning centers. Statewide master plans generally give explicit responsibility to the community colleges for providing education and counseling for adults (Cross, 1970). But most community colleges have been so swamped with the influx of undereducated recent high school graduates that they have given relatively little attention to the special needs of adults. Nevertheless, community colleges do attract a high proportion and a greater diversity of older students than any other type of institution in the educational core, and they also serve their quite traditional fare to a much greater proportion of part-time students than other postsecondary institutions.

Finally, off and on throughout history, public libraries have attempted to fill the void regarding information about educational opportunities and to play an active role in the flow of information to all interested persons—affiliated and nonaffiliated, rich and poor, educated and not educated. As early as 1926, the Commission on the Library and Adult Education appointed by the American Library Association recommended, among other things, that libraries should feel an obligation to provide reliable information about opportunities for adult education in the community (Knowles, 1962).

In conclusion, there are in reality many places that an individual can go to obtain information about educational opportunities. Few places, however, are equipped to furnish the individual with materials about a broad range of opportunities. There are even fewer that seek out potential learners to tell them of educational opportunities; most information and counseling centers presently in existence have more demand than they can handle and more information bombardment than they can keep up with. Almost no existing counseling facility feels any obligation to establish a two-way communication system that might have the potential for converting learners' requests into new opportunities.

Communications from Students. Twenty-five years ago, S. V. Martorana reported that the greatest problem in developing programs for adults in the community was the need for criteria to determine what courses to offer. Not a great deal of progress has been made in that realm. The present situation, as well as the potential promise, is aptly described by Medsker and Tillery (1971):

> A paucity of information exists about most of these older students, particularly the ones attending part

time. That they have jobs and family responsibilities and are highly motivated goes without saying, but information about their various abilities, interests, and intellectual predispositions is still needed. More than any other institution, the community college seems destined to become the most significant medium for continuing education—the educational center in its local community—but it will need data about its clients in order to do its job well [p. 49].

On the whole, however, only minor attention is being given to the two-way aspect of program development in the rash of proposals now being formulated by proponents of nontraditional studies. Some proposals fail to give explicit attention to even the most rudimentary dissemination and counseling provisions. Others do mention the development of "learning centers" but frequently conceive of them as stations that will aid students in adjusting to the requirements of traditional education. The University Without Walls (UWW), sponsored by nineteen colleges in the Union for Experimenting Colleges and Universities, stands apart for its concern with involving students in a dialogue concerning the design of educational alternatives and for its stated intention of reaching into the educational periphery and the broader community to use nontraditional learning resources. (For a description of UWW and other new proposals, see Chapter Four.)

Other bright spots in the development of innovative plans to create counseling and instructional programs that are responsive to the needs of people exist in scattered places throughout the nation. A small band of adult educators in this country have been long-time pioneers in the recognition of the need for two-way communications, and they have been working for years to establish channels of communication with potential adult learners. Some community colleges are establishing excellent links with a broad spectrum of the population in their communities; and the excitement of the evening program is unmistakable on some campuses. Another model for establishing services that reach the people exists on a state-wide basis in Utah, where eight regional service centers are expected to provide testing, counseling, referral, and other informational and instructional services as deemed appropriate by a system of task forces and advisory committees operating at the local level. Still another model is one utilizing public libraries, the Dallas Public Library Independent Study Project. This project is designed to investigate the effectiveness of the library as a center for independent study toward achieving a two-year college education by adults. The project will reach into all areas of the city, and special attention will be given to the development of five models to serve different socioeconomic groups. Colleges in the area will participate through providing multimedia presentations of their offerings. Considerable emphasis will be placed on helping adults to prepare for the College-Level Examination Program (CLEP) through study guides, reading lists, tutoring services, and workshops. A local advisory committee will provide direction in implementing the project, and a National Interest Council will review the project and consider the implications for a national program.

Although it is beyond the scope of this chapter to describe comprehensively all efforts to establish a communications network, a careful survey of ongoing activity would reveal many agencies and many communities with imaginative and innovative programs. This preliminary look at people and their needs indicates that lifelong learning is the trend of the future, that the barriers to opportunity must be removed and non-traditional programs must be improved, and that equality of access will become a reality only when people have equal opportunity to know about educational offerings and to influence the nature of those offerings.

Problems of Access

REFERENCES

COLLINS, J. W., AND WEISBERG, R. *Training Needs in Correctional Institutions.* Manpower Research Bulletin 8. Washington, D.C.: Office of Manpower Policy, Department of Labor, April 1966.

CROSS, K. P. *Beyond the Open Door: New Students to Higher Education.* San Francisco: Jossey-Bass, 1971.

CROSS, K. P. "The Role of the Junior College in Providing Postsecondary Education for All." In *Trends in Postsecondary Education.* Washington, D.C.: Office of Education, 1970, pp. 181–195.

DRUCKER, P. *This Age of Discontinuity: Guidelines to Our Changing Society.* New York: Harper and Row, 1968.

HEIST, P. (Ed.) *The Creative College Student: An Unmet Challenge.* San Francisco: Jossey-Bass, 1968.

HOBAN, C. F. *Determinants of Adult Enrollment in Televised College-Credit Courses.* Part II. Philadelphia: University of Pennsylvania, Institute for Cooperative Research, 1965.

JOHNSTONE, J. W. C., AND RIVERA, R. J. *Volunteers for Learning.* Chicago: Aldine, 1965.

KNOWLES, M. S. *The Adult Education Movement in the United States.* New York: Holt, 1962.

MATTFELD, J. A. *A Decade of Continuing Education: Dead End or Open Door.* Bronxville, N.Y.: Sarah Lawrence College, 1971. (Mimeo.)

MEDSKER, L. L., AND TILLERY, D. *Breaking the Access Barriers.* New York: McGraw-Hill, 1971.

MORTON, J. R. *University Extension in the United States.* University, Alabama: University of Alabama Press, 1953.

MOSES, S. "Notes on the Learning Force," *Notes on the Future of Education,* 1970a, *1*(2), 6–8.

MOSES, S. *The Learning Force: An Approach to the Politics of Education.* Syracuse, N.Y.: Educational Policy Research Center, Syracuse University Research Corporation, March 1970b.

K. Patricia Cross, J. Quentin Jones

OLTMAN, R. M. *Campus 1970: Where Do Women Stand?* Washington, D.C.: American Association of University Women, December 1970.

SHARON, A. T. *College Credit for Off-Campus Study.* Report 8, ERIC Clearinghouse on Higher Education. Washington, D.C.: George Washington University, March 1971.

SHELDEN, M. A., AND HEMBROUGH, B. L. *The Student Wife and the Married Woman Student: Their Educational Needs, Desires, and Backgrounds.* Urbana, Ill.: Office of the Dean of Women, University of Illinois, September 1964.

STECKLIEN, J. E., RINGO, E. N., AND MAC DONALD, J. *Students Enrolled in the TV College, General Extension Division, Fall 1965.* Minneapolis: University of Minnesota, Bureau of Institutional Research, 1966.

TROW, M. "Admissions and the Crisis in American Higher Education." In *Higher Education for Everybody?* Washington, D.C.: American Council on Education, 1970, pp. 43–48.

WHITE, M. S. (Ed.) *The Next Step: A Guide to Opportunities in Greater Boston for the Educated Woman.* Cambridge, Mass.: Radcliffe Institute for Independent Study, 1964.

WILLINGHAM, W. W. *Free-Access Higher Education.* New York: College Entrance Examination Board, 1970.

3

Ernest W. Kimmel

Problems of
Recognition

If the opportunity for lifelong learning is to be extended to much broader segments of the population than has ever before been attempted, the barriers that prohibit certain groups of people from participating fully in educational activities must be eliminated. Obviously, people do have major problems in following traditionally recognized pathways to knowledge. For some people, the mere act of presenting themselves physically in college classrooms over an extended period

64

of years is a barrier that they cannot overcome; education must be taken to them. Others find that academic credits earned in traditional ways are not transportable even within the same system of tradition. Then there are those who have the problem of a wide disparity between educational achievement and number of credits obtained. Because their leaning was accomplished in non-traditional ways, it cannot be accorded traditional recognition.

At the heart of these problems lies the traditional concept of learning and credit. No one really believes that learning and academic credits are synonymous. In reality, however, the individual who possesses the knowledge but not the degree is handicapped occupationally, economically, and in many cases even socially. Much of the nation's drive toward equality of educational opportunity has been directed toward achieving equality of access. Relatively little attention has been given to the other side of the coin, the achievement of recognition for equal levels of learning accomplishment. Chapter Three contrasts the traditional treatment of the recognition of educational achievement with some non-traditional alternatives that possess the potential for enfranchising thousands of educationally accomplished students. (Editors)

Any discussion of the evaluation and recognition of non-traditional learning must chart a careful course between a number of opposing concerns. The quality of learning is one frequently cited concern. If equality of educational recognition is to be accorded non-traditional learners, it is axiomatic that the standards of quality required of traditional learning must be upheld for non-traditional learning. Otherwise, the non-traditional learner would be receiving a debased degree or set of credentials. The entire enterprise will be successful only if a balance is maintained: individuals with non-traditional learning must be permitted to gain recognition; at the same time, respectable standards for recognition must be upheld.

Although a broad range of things are learned in non-traditional settings, this chapter will be limited to achievement that merits *academic* recognition. In other words, we will be concerned with learning that can be demonstrated to be similar to that which takes place in traditional academic settings, rather than learning which is only of recreational or occupational value. The scope of this chapter is limited further to the recognition of learning that commonly occurs at a postsecondary level. Thus, our consideration will be limited to the recognition of college-level learning that has occurred in non-traditional settings.

The forms of recognition accorded a learner—be it a grade, a number of credits, a certificate, or a degree—certify to past academic accomplishments. In the United States, as Spurr (1970) points out, "the baccalaureate does not confer the right to attend graduate school; and the law degree does not admit the holder to the bar" (p. 5). In general, this chapter will consider recognition as the process and form of certifying past achievement. It would be unrealistic, however, to ignore the likelihood that the recognition accorded to non-traditional learning will be used in the selection of people for employment or advanced education. President Curtiss (1971) of Scripps College recently posed the question "What kind of recognition will established institutions give to external degrees? Will they accept them as evidence of the qualifications of prospective students to pursue graduate and professional studies?" In his review of college grading practices, Warren (1971) found that "the most commonly discussed purpose of grades is their use as a device for screening and selecting students" (p. 27). If selection is such a dominant use of the forms of recognition among students in a traditional setting, it seems very likely that the forms of recognition accorded non-traditional learning will be used similarly.

Another force which impinges on the recognition of non-traditional learning, but which will not be treated extensively in this paper, is the recognition accorded by nonacademic agencies such as governmental and professional licensing and certifying boards. Such recognition "by professional societies or governmental bodies exists primarilly to qualify an individual for professional employment, not to measure past academic progress" (Spurr, 1970, pp. 2–3). The achievement of such occupational recognition frequently is the goal of the individuals engaged in non-traditional study, although many are barred from seeking licensing or certification because they lack the prerequisite academic credentials. Individuals will be helped to achieve their occupational goals if the forms of recognition accorded non-traditional learning are accepted by licensing or certifying agencies as meeting their academic prerequisites. There are already a number of professional certification agencies that accept a good performance on the College-Level Examination Program's General Examinations as the equivalent of their requirement for two years of college prior to taking the professional examination. The willingness of licensing and certifying agencies to accept the degrees or credits awarded for non-traditional learning will depend, in large measure, on the treatment accorded these forms of recognition by the traditional colleges and universities.

It seems useful in discussing the recognition of learning, either traditional or non-traditional, to distinguish between the *evaluation* of achievement and the *recognition* of that achievement. Evaluation consists of the variety of processes used to determine the level of knowledge or understanding that has been achieved in a particular field. Evaluation can be part of the learning process, providing both the learner and the instructor with information to assess progress to date and to guide additional study. Evaluation also can be a technique to summarize one's level of achievement at a point in time without reference to future study or instruction. Recognition consists of the limited set of symbols that formally represent the level of academic accomplishment, the collegiate "coin of the realm." The symbols of recognition (grades, advanced placement, credit hours, certificates, and degrees) condense the results of evaluation into a more manageable and interchangeable medium of exchange. A baccalaureate degree is assumed to represent a certain level of accomplishment without regard to the nature of the processes that were used to evaluate the knowledge and understanding of the recipient. It is when the separate functions of evaluation and recognition are implicitly assumed to be one that much of the fruitless debate over advanced placement, credit by examination, or external degrees occurs. The same recognition (for instance, three credits in sociology) can be appropriate even though one person was evaluated by teacher's judgments during a course and another person was evaluated by means of an external examination.

EVALUATING TRADITIONAL COLLEGE LEARNING

Many different means are used at present in evaluating college-level learning. Some of these means are quite subjective, relying on the personal judgment of the evaluator. Other means are more systematic, reducing the influence of the interpersonal relationship between learner and evaluator. The variety of means invariably tap many different dimensions of behavior and achievement. There is no agreement, however, as to which dimensions should form the basis for awarding recognition. The question turns on one's definition of what a degree, or credit toward a degree, symbolizes. Many would argue that a degree represents a certain level of academic achievement and that the only relevant means of evaluation are those which assess an individual's proficiency in academic subjects. Others would argue that, in addition to academic achievement, a baccalaureate degree symbolizes the achievements of certain personal attributes of mind and spirit. Such nonacademic attributes are difficult to evaluate, not least because there is no consensus on what they are or on appropriate criteria for judging their attainment. The evaluation of these attributes usually becomes a matter of the subjective judgment of an instructor.

Much of the resistence to the ideas of credit by examination and external degrees focusses on this concern that a degree or credit should attest to the development of certain personal traits and characteristics. The proponents of this position argue, perhaps with some validity, that these attributes cannot be evaluated unless the potential degree recipient has sat in their classrooms and has been resident on their campus. The basic question, however, is whether the attainment of these characteristics, a worthy and legitimate educational goal at certain institutions, is a necessary part of the achievement recognized by the granting of college credit, advanced placement, or the award of a degree.

Evaluation by Teachers. A teacher's judgment is an important means of evaluation within the traditional academic setting and is far from unknown in less conventional instructional situations. Although a case for separating the instructional and evaluation functions has been made repeatedly, the practice continues to be very common in American higher education. A teacher's judgment may be based on many things— some relevant to the educational goals of the student and institution, others quite irrelevant. Some teachers have been reputed to evaluate a student on the basis of his adherence to housekeeping rules. Or a teacher's evaluation may be based on a student's achievement of certain personal characteristics—for example, the poise and confidence with which the student speaks in a classroom discussion. Perhaps the most common judgmental role of a teacher is as an expert evaluating a paper or product of a student. The evaluation is frequently based both on the skill with which something is done, such as the writing of a paper or the execution of a laboratory experiment, and on the content of the paper or experiment. Such an evaluation may be impressionistic and holistic in nature; that is, the quality of the entire product is judged, without reference to specific criteria. Alternatively, some teachers may use well-defined criteria that relate to specific goals of the learning exercise, judging the product on the adequacy with which these criteria are met. The first procedure may be especially appropriate to the evaluation of creative productions such as literature, dance, sculpture, or music, where it is difficult to distinguish technique from content. The more systematic approach may be particularly applicable in situations with clearly defined behavioral or content goals. It tends to ensure that a comparable evaluation of every student is made.

Evaluation commonly used by teachers suffers from various limitations, which should be considered in relation to the purposes of the evaluation. These limitations focus around three concerns that must be considered with all types of evaluation: validity, reliability, and practicality. The validity of any evaluation has to do with the adequacy with which it measures or assesses what it is purported or intended to measure: Does it meet the purpose for which the evaluation is being made? Reliability has to do with the consistency of the evaluation: Would a student receive the same evaluation if the procedure were repeated? Practicality has to do with the usefulness of the evaluation procedure in the real world of education, where the optimal conditions assumed by psychometricians seldom seem to obtain. The constraints of practicality dictate a limit to the amount of student and teacher time that can be taken up with formal evaluation procedures and a limit to the costs of carrying out these procedures. Evaluation procedures, no matter how valid and reliable, that require sizable expenditures of time and/or money will never gain wide acceptance on college campuses.

Unless goals have been clearly defined, it is difficult to assess the validity of teachers' judgments. Because many teachers do not make their goals for the class explicit, teachers are open to the charge that their judgment of a student is capricious and personal, and therefore lacking in either validity or reliability. In making a test—be it essay, multiple-choice, or short-answer—the teacher is forced to make at least a rough statement of objectives. This provides a basis for assessing the validity of the test. Essay tests may relate to broad, integrative goals of a course but do a poor job of sampling a wide range of topics. The difficulty of grading essays is one of the chief stumbling blocks to their use. The grading requires a great deal of time on the part of the instructor and has the potential for reflecting the mood or the tiredness of the teacher. The teacher can develop a scoring guide to help achieve reliability in the grading, and additional readers can be used to help control for the personal biases of the first reader. Yet such procedures add to the time and expense of the evaluation, reducing its practicality for many situations.

A short-answer type of test allows for more questions in the same time period, thus permitting a better coverage of the material. To maintain comparability of grading among students, the instructor needs to define the criteria he will use in scoring the answers. There is little empirical evidence regarding the technical qualities of this type of item, although an investigation of its merits is currently under way at Educational Testing Service. It appears to have greater practicality than essay tests.

Much of the expense connected with objective tests

comes in the construction of the test. It takes a great deal of review and rewriting to have all of the distractors within an item functioning to discriminate between those with inaccurate or partial knowledge and those with a full understanding of the topic. The practical payoff is in the scoring, which in many institutions is done by machine, making it possible for large numbers of students to be evaluated in a comparatively short period of time and with the assurance that personal biases do not enter into the scoring.

The objective format makes it possible to sample widely from the topics relevant to the purposes of the evaluation. This same wide coverage, however, may give the impression that the test is concerned with a jumble of discrete facts, ignoring the interrelation of these facts. This impression usually results from a failure to plan the test as a coherent whole and from a failure to write test items that go beyond factual recall. The reliability of the test (as opposed to the accuracy of its scoring) varies with the number and quality of questions asked.

The choice by teachers of the evaluation procedures to be used varies with the goals of instruction and the purpose the evaluation is to serve. The quality of the evaluation is dependent on the degree to which these goals are explicitly considered in determining the criteria by which a student is tc be evaluated. Much of the criticism directed at evaluation by teachers is the result of the failure of many teachers to adequately define and plan the evaluation of the students, be it for the formative purpose of shaping further instruction or for the summative purpose of providing a basis for academic recognition.

External Examinations. In addition to the tests and other procedures made by teachers to evaluate college-level learning, there are many measures of college-level achievement produced by organizations or individuals not directly involved in the instructional process. These tend to be formal paper-and-pencil tests developed by test publishers, state departments of education, professional associations, and governmental agencies. Some of these tests are available as a well-developed testing program, such as the New York State College Proficiency Examination Program or the Graduate Record Examinations. Others (for instance, the Modern Photography Comprehension Test) are isolated, one-shot instruments. A comprehensive digest of these external examinations can be found in the *Listing of College-Level Achievement Tests* (Educational Testing Service, 1970).

The major testing programs that evaluate college-level achievement are summarized below.

The American Chemical Society's *Cooperative Examinations* provide tests in nine of the major areas of chemistry. These tests are designed to provide a professional standard for evaluating a student's competence in chemistry.

The *Achievement Tests* of the College Entrance Examination Board and the derivative *College Placement Tests* cover seventeen subject areas. Although designed to evaluate achievement at the secondary school level, these tests are frequently used by colleges in the placement of students into advanced sections or courses.

The Psychological Corporation publishes the *Achievement Tests in Nursing* series, covering fifteen major areas of a nursing curriculum.

The *Advanced Placement Program* of the College Board provides measures for evaluating college-level learning in sixteen areas. These tests, a mixture of essay and objective formats, are based on college-level courses designed to be taught in secondary school.

American College Testing Program instruments, like

the College Board's Achievement Tests, are designed to measure secondary school achievement but are frequently used for placement at the college level.

The California Achievement Tests of the California Test Bureau, McGraw-Hill, provide an evaluation of the basic skill areas of reading, arithmetic, and language.

The *College-Level Examination Program* (CLEP), sponsored by the College Board, is designed to serve credit-by-examination purposes and is based on the premise that individuals should receive recognition for what they have learned without regard to where they learned it. The examinations in this program are used by some colleges to evaluate the learning of non-traditional students, such as adults or military personnel. Other colleges use the examinations to evaluate more traditional students. The United States Armed Forces Institute makes use of certain of the CLEP examinations. To evaluate individuals, CLEP offers a battery of five General Examinations, which parallel broad general education requirements, and twenty-nine Subject Examinations, similar to end-of-course examinations in commonly taught subjects. Most of the Subject Examinations include an optional essay section, which is graded by the institution using the results. An additional five Subject Examinations are to be introduced.

The New York State Education Department sponsors the *College Proficiency Examination Program*, which, like CLEP, is directed to the idea of credit by examination. This program uses examinations in thirty-six subjects. A number of the examinations have been made specifically for CPEP; others are drawn from other programs, like Advanced Placement, CLEP, and the Modern Language Association tests.

The *Cooperative Mathematics Tests* of Educational Testing Service offer the means of evaluating competence in four college-level areas of mathematics.

The *Advanced Tests* of the Graduate Record Examinations provide a comprehensive evaluation of the topics which a student majoring in a particular field might be expected to have mastered. Examinations in twenty-one fields are offered. The results typically are used in admission to graduate school.

The *Cooperative Test Services* of Educational Testing Service offer examinations in five languages at several levels of competence. The Modern Language Association—*Cooperative Foreign Language Tests* have editions suitable for use after one and two years of college language study. These tests are appropriate to advanced students and language majors.

The National League for Nursing sponsors the *Achievement Tests for Basic Professional Nursing Program.* There are tests in nineteen areas of nursing.

The *National Teacher Examinations,* administered by Educational Testing Service, are designed to assess the competence of students preparing for a career in teaching. The results are used by school boards in selection and employment and by some states for certification. Examinations cover a student's general education and professional preparation. In addition, there are examinations in twenty-three areas of teaching specialization.

Although similar in some ways to the National Teacher Examinations, the *Teacher Education Examination Program* of Educational Testing Service is intended to serve the needs of teacher education institutions in evaluating their students. This program offers a general professional examination as well as tests in thirteen areas of teaching specialization.

The *Undergraduate Program for Counseling and Evaluation,* sponsored by Educational Testing Service, provides examinations for institutional use in institutional research, curricular evaluation, student assessment, senior comprehensives, and academic counseling and placement. There are three Area Tests quite similar to the comparable CLEP

General Examinations. The twenty-four Field Tests are similar to the Advanced Tests of the Graduate Record Examinations, mentioned above.

The United States Armed Forces Institute's *Subject Standardized Tests* are related to the comparable USAFI courses. While serving as end-of-course tests for these courses, the tests are "intended to be suitable for those who have completed any equivalent course, regardless of the specific materials used in studying the subject matter" (United States Armed Forces Institute, 1965, p. 88). There are approximately seventy Subject Standardized Tests at the college level.

Although subject to the same concerns for validity, reliability, and practicality, the external examinations used to evaluate college-level learning have a number of characteristics which distinguish them from teacher-made tests in the same fields. A very important difference is in the content of the tests. Since most of these tests are intended to be suitable for students of varying background, they are not tailored to a specific course or mode of instruction. (The Advanced Placement Examinations are an exception to this; a detailed course syllabus is provided for each test.) This need for more general applicability usually leads to the use of items that sample from a broader range of topics than would be used, typically, in a teacher-made test. In this way, every student may find himself familiar with enough topics to do creditably on the test, without having mastered every topic.

Many of these external examinations are made by a group of scholars in the particular field. Consequently, the specifications for the test tend to represent a consensus of the important topics, concepts, or skills in the field. In contrast, teacher-made tests may cover only those topics that a specific instructor finds of special interest. Therefore, the involvement of a group of scholars in defining and making an examination provides, in most cases, for a high level of content validity.

Ernest W. Kimmel

Most of the external examinations can be scored objectively and usually by machine. Even those, like the Advanced Placement Examinations, which use an essay go to great lengths (and expense) to ensure that the grading is free of capricious and idiosyncratic judgments, so that the score received is highly reliable.

The results of evaluation by an external examination are frequently reported on a score scale with certain predefined characteristics that are useful for comparisons among students or over time. The score usually receives its meaning from normative data based on a sample of students.

Most publishers of these college-level achievement tests make some effort to comply with the *Standards for Educational and Psychological Tests and Manuals* (American Psychological Association, 1966). Consequently, information about the technical qualities of a test is available to the potential user, so that he can judge the evidence for the reliability and validity of the test.

Use of Normative Approach. All of the externally made examinations and most of the evaluation procedures used by teachers judge the competence or achievement of an individual by comparing his performance with that of some group. When evaluated by his teacher, an individual's performance frequently is compared with that of other students who happen to be taking the same course that term. Teachers who use the same test year after year may have comparative data based on the students of previous years. The test publishers usually provide comparative data to the user. These data may be based on an undefined group of students who were used to "try out" one test, or on the students who took the test in a given period of time, or on a sample of students chosen to represent a certain defined population. Colleges may also develop normative data from the performance of their own students on these tests.

Problems of Recognition

This *normative* approach, comparing the performance of an individual with that of some group of students, has characterized almost all measurement in American education. Most of the techniques of educational measurement have been developed to increase our ability to distinguish between the performances of different individuals, so that they can be ranked. Recently, however, there has been considerable criticism of the normative approach. Many of the ills of American education have been blamed on this approach, which, by definition, classifies some individuals as below average—that is, as "failures." The suggested alternative is that individuals be evaluated in ways that will permit statements about their knowledge or mastery of a field without reference to the level of mastery achieved by anyone else. This would enable every student to learn at his own rate, proceeding to new material when he is ready, not when the "average" student of a particular college is ready.

The development of such *criterion-referenced* or *absolute-standard* tests has many implications for the instructional process as well as for the process of evaluation. Such tests are built into most of the experiments with "individualized" or "individually prescribed" instruction. The test itself becomes the criterion against which an individual's performance is judged. Most of these experiments are being conducted at the elementary or secondary level. There have been only a few scattered attempts with isolated courses to apply these ideas at the college level. These attempts have usually been in the context of developing instructional strategies using contemporary technology. No one has attempted to develop an entire degree program based on these ideas. Such an attempt would involve a clearer and more detailed statement of the knowledge and skills represented by the awarding of a degree than any institution has made to date.

Ernest W. Kimmel

RECOGNITION OF TRADITIONAL COLLEGE LEARNING

Many forms of recognition exist today in American higher education. In most cases recognition is awarded on the basis of the evaluation made of an individual student. The recognition derives its worth, however, from the institution awarding it, and from the quality ascribed to that institution by accrediting associations and governmental agencies, as well as by the broader educational world. The most common form of recognition accorded a student is a grade. Grading practices and the forms of grades vary immensely. Grading systems range from numerical scales which make many distinctions to a pass-fail (or no record) system which has only two levels. All grades are based on some kind of evaluation, and most grading systems provide differential recognition according to the level of competency shown by the student during the evaluation.

Since grades are commonly awarded by individual teachers, they have no standard meaning. The meaning is dependent on the evaluation procedure as well as the topic being evaluated. In addition, different teachers may recognize the same level of demonstrated competence with different grades. This "meaninglessness" of grades has been one of the arguments used by proponents of the more generalized pass-fail grading system. Such a system is, in effect, equivalent to another form of recognition, the awarding (or recording) of credit. In simplest terms, credits, as used here, are the bookkeeping units which symbolize the amount of education a student has accumulated. These units may be expressed in number of courses, semester hours, or quarter hours; but all are quantitative measures of a student's education.

These quantitative units are commonly awarded to a

79

student for completing a specified amount of instruction with at least a minimal level of achievement as symbolized by the instructor-assigned grade. Many institutions will also award credit if a minimal level of achievement is demonstrated on an examination. Traditionally, this examination has been the responsibility of the faculty of the institution awarding the credit. In some institutions there have been well-developed, well-publicized programs encouraging students to take examinations for credit. In other institutions credit by examination is mentioned in the fine print of the catalog, but students have difficulty finding any faculty member willing to do the evaluation.

In recent years, three testing programs have been developed to evaluate a student's knowledge and to provide the results to an institution as basis for awarding credit. These testing programs, mentioned in the previous section, are the Advanced Placement Program and the College-Level Examination Program of the College Entrance Examination Board, and the College Proficiency Examination Program of the New York State Department of Education. With these testing programs providing the evaluation, at the monetary expense of the student, the incidence of credit being awarded by examination has increased. The institutions and their faculties still are responsible for determining the minimal score level for which credit will be awarded.

Even though credits would seem to be the simplest form of recognition, they still do not represent a universal medium of exchange within the higher-education system. The credits awarded by one institution are not always accepted by another institution if the student decides to transfer. A recent study of transfer students shows that 13 per cent of these students lost at least one semester's accumulation of credits when they transferred to a second college.

Although no credits are awarded, previous learning is

sometimes recognized by the placement of a student into a more advanced course. While this enables a student to avoid sitting through a course for which he has already mastered the material, it does not increase his accumulated credits toward a degree. Placement is frequently based on the same kinds of evaluation as credit by examination. In some situations it represents a lower level of performance than the award of credit; in others, it becomes the institution's substitute for credit by examination.

From the perspective of the individual student, the most important form of academic recognition is the award of a degree or certificate. Advanced placement, grades, or credit hours are just milestones along the way. Unless the degree is received, the credits and grades serve little purpose. Employers do not ask, "How many credits have you accumulated?" but rather, "Do you have a degree or certificate?"

There are several levels and hundreds of names for the degrees presently available (Spurr, 1970); but within the scope of undergraduate education two degree levels are most widely accepted: the *associate's* degree, universally used for the successful completion of two years of undergraduate studies in college—whether in liberal arts or in technical or vocational subjects; and the *bachelor's* degree, given for satisfactory completion of a four-year undergraduate program. The chief feature of the definition of academic degrees is the length of time served, not the quality of achievement represented by the award of a degree (although many institutions do recognize the qualitative difference in the achievement of certain students by awarding the degree *with honors* or by election to an honor society such as Phi Beta Kappa). In addition to the total amount of time served, a degree usually attests to a certain amount of time served at the specific institution awarding the degree.

Although this definition of associate and bachelor's

degrees in terms of time served leaves much to be desired, it is, realistically, about the only common meaning of the degrees awarded by different institutions. The lack of a common meaning to the degrees or certificates awarded by different institutions reflects the great variation among institutions of higher education. American colleges and universities vary in size from less than a hundred to tens of thousands of students; they range from single-purpose institutions to vast multipurpose universities; and, most important to the meaning of a degree or certificate, they vary widely in the background and quality of the students and faculty which they attract to their campuses. The respect accorded a degree by graduate schools, employers, and the general public depends, at least in part, on the perceived quality of the student body and the faculty that provides the instruction.

In order to assure a minimal standard of quality, most traditional institutions of higher education have sought accreditation from their respective regional accrediting association and from appropriate specialized professional accrediting associations. The accrediting associations have been accused of ignoring the public interest and being one of the most powerful forces resisting change in higher education (Koerner, 1971). Yet these voluntary organizations have played a large role in maintaining quality within a diverse educational system, and without the homogenizing effect of government-imposed standards. Their test will come in adapting to the changes in higher education during the next few years. The traditional institutions represented in the accrediting associations no longer have a monopoly on providing postsecondary academic instruction. Even the limited control of quality exercised through the accrediting associations could easily be lost if they do not broaden their viewpoint and thus the range of institutions and educational agencies that can be candidates for accreditation.

This variation in the quality of institutions and the

respect accorded their degrees is partly caused by the wide variation among the several states in the legal requirements to become a degree-granting institution. Although most states have adopted reasonable standards for chartering an institution, some states appear to have been excessively generous in giving out the right to grant degrees.

None of the forms of recognition currently awarded by academic institutions have a meaning which extends to all students or all institutions. Grades and credits reflect the idiosyncratic policies and practices of individual instructors or institutions. The meaning of a degree, other than as a measure of the amount of time served, is dependent on the characteristics of the institution awarding it. Although the accrediting associations monitor a minimal level of quality in traditional institutions, they do not control the wide range in quality above that minimum, nor do they accredit all possible sources of instruction or all institutions that are legally empowered to award a degree.

Beyond the academic world, the individual frequently must seek recognition from a state or professional licensing or certifying agency before he can gain employment to use what he has learned. In some states and in some fields, an individual's certification may be based on the college's attesting to his preparation in the field: "Because he graduated from the program at XYZ college, he meets our standards." In other situations, certification or licensure depends on the individual's having accumulated the right combination of credits: "Six of these, and three of those, and eighteen of something else." In still other fields, the licensing or certifying body conducts its own evaluation, usually via a written examination, before granting its form of recognition to the individual. Even in this situation, some form of recognition by an academic institution (accumulated credits or a degree) is a frequent prerequisite.

In American higher education there is no single pattern through which learning is evaluated and recognized. The standards used in evaluation are set by the individual institution and, commonly, by the individual instructor within that institution. Although the recognition accorded college-level learning gives the external appearance of reasonable uniformity, the value ascribed to it varies greatly, usually as a function of the reputation of the institution at which it was granted.

EVALUATING NON-TRADITIONAL LEARNING

The evaluation of non-traditional learning involves many of the same problems as the evaluation of learning in traditional situations. Provision must be made both to evaluate the achievement of individuals and to evaluate and accredit some of the programs and means of instruction through which learning takes place.

Any procedures for evaluating the individual non-traditional learner must meet acceptable standards of validity, reliability, and practicality. Poor evaluation procedures will provide an inadequate base for an acceptable and respected form of recognition.

Evaluating non-traditional learners presents a number of unique problems when compared with the evaluation of students in traditional educational institutions. Some problems are logistical in nature; non-traditional learners usually do not physically assemble. Those to be evaluated may be scattered throughout a city, a state, or the entire nation or in other countries. An entire delivery system will need to be built to ensure that the learning of any individual can be evaluated without regard to his geographical location or mobility.

Another complication in evaluating non-traditional learning is that of defining the subject or topic on which the individual is to be evaluated in such a way that it is not dependent on a particular textbook or instructional approach. This will require a broadly based and scholarly consensus on what should be evaluated.

The range of possible subjects or competencies to be evaluated is probably much wider than the range of course offerings in most traditional institutions. Thus, the system for evaluating non-traditional learning will need great breadth if it is to be responsive to the needs of non-traditional learners. At the same time, much of non-traditional learning will not be easily compartmentalized into the neat little packages dictated by the calendar of traditional colleges and universities. A truly responsive system for evaluating non-traditional learning will have to cope with units of evaluation which vary in scope and length.

The external examinations that already exist (see pp. 73–76 above) provide a valuable base from which to develop the means of evaluating individual non-traditional learners. The CLEP General Examinations and Undergraduate Program Area Tests provide measures of achievement in broad general education areas similar to the broad distribution requirements of many college curricula. The CLEP Subject Examinations, the CPEP tests, and the USAFI Subject Standardized Tests, the Psychological Corporation's Achievement Tests in Nursing, and other tests provide the means of evaluating many discrete subjects organized in a fashion which tends to parallel the traditional college courses. The Field Tests of the Undergraduate Program and the NTE tests of fields of teaching specialization provide the means of evaluating an individual's command of an academic discipline at a level comparable to that expected of a student majoring in that discipline. One of the first steps to be taken in developing a system of evaluation is for each of these existing tests to be reviewed to determine its suitability, both in content and in psychometric characteristics, for use with non-traditional learners.

Problems of Recognition

Although existing examinations can form a starting point in developing the means of evaluating non-traditional learning, they are insufficient both in the range of topics covered and in the techniques used for evaluation. Following the review of existing examinations, a second study should be initiated to identify the fields of study and areas of competency that will need to the evaluated. This study should examine the needs of our society for developing manpower in certain critical areas (for instance, in the health professions) as well as identifying those fields (computer programming, for instance) where a substantial number of people pursue their studies outside of traditional collegiate institutions. The study should identify the areas served by suitable existing examinations as well as those areas where new means of evaluation must be developed. This study should also attempt to estimate the number of potential candidates for recognition in each area.

In addition, serious attention should be given to the criterion problem. What is an appropriate basis for judging whether or not someone has mastered a particular subject? We have commented above on the problems connected with the traditional normative approach—judging an individual's accomplishments by reference to the distribution of performances within some group. In addition to the theoretical and philosophical concerns surrounding the normative approach, there will be some very practical problems in relying exclusively on this approach in evaluating non-traditional learning. As suggested below, the evaluation of non-traditional learning will undoubtedly involve "made-to-order" examinations or other forms of evaluation. The choice of a standard or criterion for judging a performance will have strong financial implication in such cases, because a sizeable portion of the expense of making most objective tests is in the standardization; that is, in converting individual performances to a score scale with particular attributes and in collecting data on a normative population to provide the basis for judging an individual's score. Since the logistical difficulties of collecting normative data in some areas will be almost insurmountable, other bases for judging an individual's performance must be developed. This may mean the use of an absolute standard, which would make it possible to describe and judge the performance of an individual even though the evaluation instrument was used only with him. It may mean the development of an entirely different basis for measurement. Clearly, a concentrated effort is needed to develop adequate alternatives to the normative approach.

The evaluation of non-traditional learning will require not only a variety of criteria for judging an individual's performance but a variety of techniques through which his achievement can be demonstrated. Some subjects or areas may best be evaluated by objective tests, either those already existing or others to be made for this purpose. Because of the expense involved in making an objective test, this technique will be most applicable to subjects in which a large number of people will seek evaluation. Other subjects or areas of learning may require the use of short-answer or essay examinations. This choice may be dictated by the content or by the infrequency of the demand for certain topics. So that the demand for evaluation in uncommon areas can be met, the problems connected with generating examinations-to-order need to be studied.

Evaluation of non-traditional learning must not be confined to examinations. Many things worthy of recognition can be demonstrated only through some type of performance measure. This would include a performance in a laboratory or on the dramatic stage. The evaluation of laboratory skill and technique might, for example, require an entire weekend, with an experienced evaluator observing the student's handling of a standard series of laboratory problems. Similarly, it might involve a defined dramatic or musical performance or the writing of a theme within certain time limits.

Problems of Recognition

Other performance measures would be needed in non-standard settings: the writing of a play, the preparation of a thesis, or the invention of a technological device. The creations to be evaluated might be similar to products frequently required in traditional courses, but should not be limited to such things. The educational outcome of two years of experience as a Peace Corps community organizer, for example, cannot be judged in the same terms as the outcome of a few one-day field trips taken as part of a traditional sociology course. The choice of product or performance to evaluate, and the way in which it is evaluated, must relate to the way in which the knowledge was gained.

New or seldom used means of evaluation will be required in some of these areas. Many of the products may require the use of panels of experts to provide the evaluation. Procedures will be needed to ensure that the judgments of panels of such experts are reliable and based on clearly defined criteria. There should be experimentation with other forms of evaluation, such as peer, supervisor, or self-ratings. As contemporary technology provides new media for instruction, these same means may be usable in the evaluation process. Audio recordings are already used in language evaluation, and they have applicability in other areas. Videotape cassettes, on-line computer terminals, or tape recorders may prove useful in the evaluation procedure.

All the means of evaluation envisaged above are not presently available. Such a fully developed system for evaluating non-traditional learning requires extended research to develop suitable measurement procedures. Once procedures are developed, a continuing mechanism is needed to carry out the evaluation of non-traditional learners. All parties would benefit by the coordination of these efforts. First, to prevent unfruitful duplication of the needed research and development. Second, to provide a single point of contact with which an individual can deal in seeking to have his learning evaluated. (All but the most tenacious individual would be discouraged if he had to turn to organization A for evaluation in the liberal arts, to organization B for evaluation in other areas, and to organization C or D for performance evaluation.) Third, to increase the chances of colleges and universities granting recognition based on the evaluation of non-traditional learning by providing the results in a systematic way. Few colleges will make the effort to understand and use the results from many sources.

How such coordination can be achieved is still an open question. Existing organizations are exploring the feasibility of assuming the responsibility for developing and coordinating a system of evaluation. Others concerned with this problem are proposing that a new nongovernmental organization be created to coordinate activities in the non-traditional study area, while yet others are predicting increased government involvement in this area of education.

While our focus has been on the evaluation of individual achievement, a question should be raised regarding the role accrediting agencies should play in the evaluation of sources of instruction outside the traditional academic community. Non-traditional study is frequently beyond the scope of current accreditation policies. Would the public be better protected if the voluntary accrediting groups broadened their activities to include non-traditional sources of instruction?

RECOGNITION OF NON-TRADITIONAL COLLEGE LEARNING

No single form of recognition will serve the needs of those with non-traditional learning. Some may demonstrate competence that should be recognized by the awarding of a degree. Others may master material equivalent to some portion of typical college curricula but less than that represented by a degree. Still others may seek recognition in terms of occupational certification or advancement.

While there is, as yet no accepted definition of the forms of recognition to be accorded non-traditional study, certain considerations are apparent. First, each evaluation procedure should be clearly designated as covering some portion of the requirements for a particular form of recognition, such as a degree. The amount of credit awarded does not have to be the same for every evaluation. Some evaluations may lead to three credit hours of recognition, while others may be designed to cover material that merits the award of credit equivalent to an entire year of full-time college study. Second, any degrees or certificates awarded in recognition of non-traditional learning must be indistinguishable from those awarded for traditional class attendance. A special degree or other academic recognition for non-traditional learning would be treated as second class by many people and many institutions regardless of the quality of work demonstrated in the process of gaining it. Consequently, the non-traditional learner would be little better off and, perhaps, worse off than before. In addition, special non-traditional forms of academic recognition would continue the proliferation of separately named degrees with their emphasis on narrow certification rather than preparation for work and life. The Carnegie Commission on Higher Education (1971, p. 23), in suggesting that the present 1600 degrees be reduced to less than 160 differently named degrees, argues that fewer degrees will lessen the chances for students to get locked in to a narrow career channel from which there are few alternative paths if one's goals and interests change.

Third, there is a need for forms of recognition other than those accorded by the academic community. Many non-traditional learners are concerned with meeting professional or occupational requirements. If the individual wants only occupational recognition, the evaluation procedures should be useable by licensing or certifying agencies as a basis for awarding their forms of recognition without the prior step of academic recognition.

A major question is who should accord the recognition. Should the monopoly of present institutions in the recognition of learning be preserved, or are new institutions and a new structure needed? As with the traditional forms of academic recognition, the status of the institution awarding recognition for non-traditional learning will, in large measure, determine the respect accorded that recognition. Many individuals would benefit if existing bellwether institutions were to provide recognition for non-traditional learning. State educational agencies —the New York Board of Regents, for example—are becoming directly involved in providing recognition for non-traditional study. This expanded role for an existing public agency provides a challenge to the monopoly of existing colleges and universities.

A number of critics have argued that it is not sufficient to get existing institutions or agencies to broaden the basis on which they recognize learning or award degrees, the monopoly of the traditional institutions needs to be broken by the creation of entirely new institutions to serve the evaluation or the recognition function or both. Newman (1971, p. 88) suggests the creation of "new Regional Examining Universities. These institutions would be credentialing and examining institutions alone—they would not offer courses but would administer examinations and grant degrees." Arbolino and Valley (1970a, 1970b, 1970c) present rather detailed objectives for what they have called variously "A National Commission for the Certification of Accomplishment in Higher Education" or "The National University." They argue that, in addition to several evaluative and information-providing functions, "The National University" should grant college-level credits and award

91

degrees in its own name. The competition of the educational marketplace will probably play an important role in determining the viability of such new institutions.

While our attention has been focused on the non-traditional learner, we should not lose sight of the benefits to our society of providing recognition for demonstrated achievement without regard to where the learning occurred. Manpower needs in key sectors of our society could be met more easily than they now are if individuals received their credentials (both academic and occupational) based on demonstrated achievement rather than on number of hours spent in class. For example, many health manpower needs could be filled quickly if recently discharged medical corpsmen could translate their medical training and experience into credentials that would be acceptable in civilian hospitals, without having to take college courses covering material already mastered. Similarly, increased flexibility could be introduced into the American work force if people were helped to new careers by being able to demonstrate the relevant skills and knowledge they already possess, rather than having to take an entire program designed for someone with no relevant previous experience or education.

Although difficult to quantify, the effect on our society of having more citizens gain personal satisfaction and fulfillment through the increased options opened by marketable credentials is an important consideration. Such citizens are in a better position to join the mainstream of our society or to challenge the direction it is taking.

It is difficult to identify the effects on the higher education system if non-traditional learning were to be accorded recognition on a par with learning gained in traditional ways. The Newman (1971, p. 88) commentary predicts that breaking the monopoly on traditional degree-granting "will also ease many of the pressures at the colleges caused by concern for obtaining a degree rather than an education." If performance or demonstrated achievement, rather than the length of time served, becomes the basis for awarding academic recognition, many colleges and universities may be forced to alter their practices in evaluating and rewarding their traditional students. This change could even lead to rethinking the college curriculum to define educational objectives susceptible to publicly observable standards for evaluation. Rather than debasing higher education, the recognition of non-traditional learning might bring many rigidly traditional colleges and universities to a renewed concern for quality and relevance in teaching and learning in our rapidly changing society.

REFERENCES

American Psychological Association. *Standards for Educational and Psychological Tests and Manuals.* Washington, D.C.: American Psychological Association, 1966.

ARBOLINO, J. N., AND VALLEY, J. R. "Education: The Institution or the Individual," *Continuing Education,* 1970a, *3*(4), 6, 55.

ARBOLINO, J. N., AND VALLEY, J. R. *The Need, the Issues, and the Strategy: A Companion Paper to A Plan for the Study of the Promise and the Problems of an External Degree.* Princeton, N.J.: Educational Testing Service, 1970b.

ARBOLINO, J. N., AND VALLEY, J. R. *A Plan for the Study of the Promise and the Problems of an External Degree.* Princeton, N.J.: Educational Testing Service, 1970c.

Carnegie Commission on Higher Education. *Less Time, More Options: Education Beyond the High School.* New York: McGraw-Hill, 1971.

CURTISS, M. H. "Higher Education in the Age of 'Future Shock.'" Paper given at annual meeting of the Western College Association, Santa Barbara, March 1971.

Educational Testing Service. *Listing of College-Level Achieve-*

ment Tests. Princeton, N.J.: Educational Testing Service, 1970.

FURNISS, W. T. "Degrees for Nontraditional Students: An Approach to New Models," *A.C.E. Special Report*, April 9, 1971.

KOERNER, J. D. "Preserving the Status Quo: Academia's Hidden Cartel," *Change*, 1971, *3*(2), 50–54.

National Commission on Accrediting. *A Proposal for a National Study of Accrediting Agencies Serving Public and Private (Including Proprietary) Education.* Washington, D.C.: National Commission, June 1970. (Mimeo.)

NEWMAN, F., et al. *Report on Higher Education.* Washington, D.C.: Department of Health, Education, and Welfare, March 1971.

PUFFER, C. E., et al. *A Report on Institutional Accreditation in Higher Education.* Chicago: Federation of Regional Accrediting Commissions of Higher Education, 1970.

SHARON, A. T. *College Credit for Off-Campus Study.* Report 8, ERIC Clearinghouse on Higher Education. Washington, D.C.: George Washington University, March 1971.

SOLOMON, R. J. "Giving Credit Where It's Due," *Educational Record*, 1970, *51*(3), 301–304.

SPURR, S. H. *Academic Degree Structures: Innovative Approaches.* New York: McGraw-Hill, 1970.

TURNER, C. P. (Ed.) *A Guide to the Evaluation of Educational Experiences in the Armed Services.* Washington, D.C.: American Council on Education, 1968.

United States Armed Forces Institute. *Catalog.* (14th ed.) Madison, 1965.

WARREN, J. R. *College Grading Practices: An Overview.* Research Bulletin 71-12. Princeton, N.J.: Educational Testing Service, 1971.

Western Interstate Commission for Higher Education. *Outputs of Higher Education: Their Identification, Measurement, and Evaluation.* Boulder, Colorado: WICHE, 1970.

4

John R. Valley

External Degree
Programs

In *American higher education there is no single pattern by which learning is evaluated and accorded recognition.
There is no real standard for the college degree. The symbols
of recognition—credit hours, advanced placement, grades, and
degrees—are arrived at through a variety of evaluation procedures. Perhaps the one aspect of the recognition system that
is most deeply embedded in tradition is the notion that institutions reserve the right to determine the requirements and*

standards for their own credits and degrees. Institutions of higher education have traditionally permitted faculty members considerable freedom in evaluating the achievement of individual students. And, within certain guidelines, voluntary accrediting associations have permitted institutions latitude in setting the standards for degrees. While the traditional system has afforded institutionalized education a certain amount of independence, it has permitted individual students relatively little control over their educational destinies.

Much of the present reform movement in American higher education is taking place at the institutional level. Many colleges and universities are exploring new ways of extending their services and instructional facilities to broader segments of the population. Some have devised new administrative procedures for the delivery of rather traditional fare. Others have created new modes of learning, as they offer non-traditional curricula that are specifically designed to meet the needs of previously excluded populations. The enthusiasm for introducing new forms of recognition for educational achievement does not stop with new structures and new programs of study. The awarding of a college degree based solely upon student performance on examinations will soon be introduced in New York. Departing even further from tradition are proposals to validate the total learning experiences of students by a great variety of methods. Whenever the student amasses the experiences that meet the institution's conception of the degree, the degree would be awarded.

There are in existence now a few well-established programs leading to external degrees; many more proposals are in the discussion or developmental stages. Chapter Four takes a systematic look at the great variety of approaches to external degree programs. Conceptually, the programs being talked about can be described as variations of six basic models. Each model is described and illustrated in Chapter Four. (Editors)

John R. Valley

In an address at the annual meeting of the College
Entrance Examination Board in October 1970, Alan Pifer,
President of the Carnegie Corporation, asked if the time had
come for an external degree in America. His presentation included an analysis of the experiences of others with external
degrees, and he encouraged experimentation with different
varieties of external degree programs. Mr. Pifer's suggestion
was offered at a time when Open University was attracting
worldwide attention and when Ewald B. Nyquist, the Commissioner of Education of the State of New York, had indicated his support for a plan for a degree to be offered by the
New York Regents upon successful performance on examinations. This mounting interest thus gave rise to a need for a
better understanding of the possibilities inherent in the concept of an external degree.

This chapter is an attempt to call attention to the
substantial range of non-traditional approaches to academic
degrees and to systematically organize these approaches into
six major models of external degree programs. (See also
Travers, 1969).

ADMINISTRATIVE-FACILITATION MODEL

The simplest—and probably the most common—
model of an external degree is the administrative-facilitation
model. Perhaps because it shares many characteristics of traditional degree programs, many do not recognize it as an external degree. However, because it is earned outside the central structure of the university, it can be legitimately regarded
as an external degree.

The administrative-facilitation model can be described
as follows: A degree-granting and instructional institution or
agency establishes an organization and/or facilities to serve the

needs of a different clientele, yet it holds to its customary degree pattern. Examples of this model are legion. Universities that have implemented this model of an external degree have proceeded to establish an evening school or an evening college as a separate administrative entity. The target audience of the instructional program is typically the adults residing in the community where the institution is located. The student group is a commuting population. Special counseling and advisory services are provided and at times that meet the needs of the clientele. Courses are offered after normal hours of employment in the evening or on Saturday. Registration can be handled by mail. Class periods are extended—one three-hour class session per week instead of three one-hour sessions. At commencement the successful candidates are presented to the president of the university by the dean of the evening college to receive their degrees. When this model has been used successfully, there is not only a recognition of the needs of a different clientele, but the institution is able to bring about an identification of this clientele with the institution.

Lest one point be missed in the preceding description, let it be highlighted. In this model the institution holds to its normal degree pattern. Thus, the changes that need to be made to create the external degree in this instance consist of assembling the services, organizational structures, and procedures that enable a new or different clientele to meet the university's regular degree requirements. This has been frequently accomplished by the setting up of a new administrative unit—frequently, but not always, called the evening college. Examples of this approach are seen in the Bachelor of Science in General Studies offered by the Evening College of the University of Cincinnati and the Bachelor of Science offered by the School of General Studies at Columbia University.

In recent years institutions have established administrative-facilitation models of external degrees by taking advantage of modern technological developments—television, video recordings, and audio tape cassettes in particular. The TV College of the Chicago Junior College System, for example, has been operating since 1956. By the medium of television, this college makes it possible for students in the Chicago area to receive in their own homes the basic instruction needed to qualify for an A.A. degree. Another example of the administrative-facilitation model built on imaginative use of modern technology is the Stanford University master's degree program in engineering. In this instance instruction is brought to students in classrooms located on business and industrial sites in the San Francisco and Berkeley areas of California. Students at these remote locations can also talk with and question their instructors via telephonic links with the on-campus class. Another illustration is the University of South Carolina televised Master in Business Administration degree program. This program makes use of the closed-circuit television network of the South Carolina Educational Television Center. Facilities of the university's regional campuses and classrooms at technical education centers and high schools are used as outlets in approximately a dozen locations throughout the state. Leased telephone lines provide talkback links to the live classroom. There are also five on-campus class meetings that begin on a Friday afternoon and continue through Saturday noon. Colorado State University, on the other hand, offers students an opportunity to earn a Master of Science degree in atmospheric, civil, electrical, industrial, or mechanical engineering via video tapes made of on-campus classes. These tapes are delivered several times each week by courier to play-back units located in industrial offices in the area. Students not only can watch a recording of the class presentation, but they can also arrange for repeat showings and make-up showings if they missed a class because of a business trip.

Electronics is not the only technological development

that has encouraged external degrees. The book, the pen or pencil, and the postal service have been used for years to enable students to qualify for external degrees. The administrative-facilitation model of external degree includes the use of correspondence instruction as the device whereby students can meet the requirements of the customary degree pattern. In 1970, at six of the fifteen Australian universities, external degrees could be earned by students who would complete their requirements largely by correspondence. In the latest year for which enrollment figures were available, there were approximately 7,000 external students enrolled in these universities (*Commonwealth Universities Yearbook,* 1970, p. 10).

MODES-OF-LEARNING MODEL

In the modes-of-learning model a degree-granting and instructional institution or agency establishes a new degree pattern of learning and teaching that seeks to adjust to the capacities, circumstances, and interests of a different clientele from that which it customarily serves. Examples of this model have existed for several years in the fairly numerous special degree programs for adults. Among the better-known programs are the Bachelor of Liberal Studies degree and the Master of of Liberal Studies degree offered by the College of Continuing Education at the University of Oklahoma, the Bachelor of General Studies degree offered by the Division of Continuing Education at Roosevelt University, the Bachelor of Independent Studies degree offered by the Center for Continuing Education at the University of South Florida, and the Bachelor of Arts in Liberal Studies offered by University College at Syracuse University. Brigham Young University (Bachelor of Independent Studies Program) and the State University College at Brockport (Bachelor of Arts in Liberal Studies) also have announced programs that fit the model.

It might be informative to examine one illustration of this model in some detail. The Bachelor of Independent Studies Adult Degree Program (BIS) of the University of South Florida will serve this purpose. The university has issued a special brochure (entitled *Bachelor of Independent Studies Adult Degree Program*) for the BIS program. The regular Bachelor of Arts (B.A.) program is described in the university's general catalog (University of South Florida, 1969). The following details were obtained from these two informational pieces.

Administratively the BIS program and the B.A. program are within the College of Liberal Arts. The university has been careful to point out that the two programs have somewhat different goals. The goals of the College of Liberal Arts are as follows:

> (1) To help students continue the exploration of new subjects according to fresh ideas and talents enriching to life. (2) To enable students to try out several fields as a means of determining the wisest vocational choice. (3) To give sufficient development within the chosen vocational field that the student will be prepared to obtain a job upon graduation or move successfully into a graduate or professional school. (4) To collaborate with the other colleges of the university in providing liberal courses to reinforce required training in those professional schools. (5) To cultivate independent thinking, creative imagination, and value commitment in order that students may become constructive leaders in their chosen activities [Catalog, p. 103].

The goals for the BIS degree are as follows:

> Through reading, writing, listening, reflection, discussion, and other avenues of learning that constitute a

101

part of the BIS Program, the adult student is expected to attain an appropriate level of understanding regarding (1) his own personality, problems, and potential; (2) an historical view of man's development—social, intellectual, scientific, artistic, and religious; (3) other individuals and groups, and a knowledge of his own and other contemporary cultures; (4) the humanities, natural sciences, social sciences, and their interrelationships; (5) the probable direction and effect of political, economic, and technological change [Brochure, p. 1].

Further, the university has established special admissions requirements for BIS applicants. That is, in addition to the general requirements for admission to the university, BIS applicants must be 25 years of age or older and must be able to provide "sufficient reasons for being unable to dedicate a block of time as a resident to complete the regular degree program" (Brochure, p. 2).

The registration fee and tution for the four-year B.A. program for an in-state student is $1,500; for an out-of-state student these fees total $2,400. University fees for the BIS degree total $2,110; and this total cost includes elements that are not shared in common with the B.A. degree fees.

Interesting as these differences are, the essence of the BIS program as an illustration of the modes-of-learning model is seen when one focuses on the degree requirements and compares these requirements with those for the B.A. degree. For the B.A. degree the College of Liberal Arts indicates that a degree candidate must fulfill the following requirements:

(1) Complete 180 quarter credits with at least a C average in work done at the university. At least 60

John R. Valley

credits must be for upper-level work. (2) Complete a general education requirement of seven courses in the College of Basic Studies—including eight credits in Functional English and three credits in Senior Seminar: Freedom and Responsibility (dealing with contemporary issues affecting social and personal values). (3) Demonstrate proficiency in four physical education areas. (4) Complete a major of 60 credits. (5) Complete his last 45 credits in residence at the university. (6) Pass a senior achievement test [Catalog, p. 104].

For the BIS degree candidate, the university expresses its degree requirements in entirely different terms (Brochure, p. 2). For these candidates the curriculum is divided into four parts: the humanities, the natural sciences, the social sciences, and inter-area studies. There is no set order for studying in these areas except that the first three listed precede the fourth. The sequence of study is determined by the individual's ability; and the rate or pace is based on the individual's experience, previous learning, and the amount of time he can devote to study. The enrollment and admission of BIS candidates can take place at any time. The university expectation is that from two to eight years might be a reasonable period in which to complete the degree requirements.

Two major phases comprise the work in each of the four areas: guided independent study and an area seminar. In the first phase, the student works under the guidance of a faculty advisor. The student works at home, but he is required to have certain minimal contacts with his advisor. When the student and his advisor feel he is ready, the student takes an area comprehensive examination. The second phase, the area seminar, follows upon successful completion of the comprehensive examination. The seminars are periods of intensive residential learning on campus of three weeks in length (the inter-area studies seminar is four weeks long) under the direction of a team of university faculty members.

In reviewing the above comparisons of the requirement for the BIS and B.A. degrees, note especially that the degree pattern for BIS candidates is very different from that of the B.A. degree and is adjusted to the circumstances, interests, and capacities of a new clientele—namely, adults.

In 1971 three other examples of the modes-of-learning model (the National Urban Studies Program, The British Open University, and the University Without Walls) attracted considerable attention. The external degree program sponsored by the Department of Housing and Urban Development (HUD) and a second program sponsored by the Union for Experimenting Colleges and Universities (UECU) both have been referred to as the "University Without Walls." Since the official name for the HUD program is the National Urban Studies Program, we will use that title here and reserve the "University Without Walls" for the UECU project.

The National Urban Studies Program (Department of Housing and Urban Development, 1970) is intended to promote the subprofessional and professional training and development of full-time federal, state, and local government employees It prepares individuals for graduate as well as undergraduate degrees. Special curricula have been developed by the participating colleges, and it is this characteristic that makes the National Urban Studies Program an illustration of the modes-of-learning model.

Government employees are instructed at local facilities or at their place of employment under schedules that take into account the employees' job responsibilities. Courses are taught intensively for one-week, three-day, or two-day sessions; assignments and course outlines are available well in advance. The plan includes the use of equivalency examinations and recognition of work experience for credit. Provision is made for complete compatibility and exchange of credit among all institutions participating in the program. Student learning packages are to be developed to include cassette-recorded lectures, tape-slide presentations, video tapes, and movies. Substantial use is made of independent study. As of January 1971, five thousand students were involved in the programs. The institutions participating in the National Urban Studies Program are the University of Northern Colorado, University of Detroit, University of Oklahoma, and Manatee Junior College. Shaw University and Morgan State University are also assisting.

The University Without Walls (UWW) is the title of a general project (Union for Experimenting Colleges and Universities, 1971) that is being implemented differently by each of the twenty institutions participating in the program. UWW involves students in a planned and continuing relationship with a residential college or university. However, for the students who elect to participate, the path to the degree is not via courses completed in standard instructional modes. For this reason UWW can serve to illustrate the many variations of the second model of external degrees.

In UWW the following ideas are considered basic to any specific program that might develop on any one of the twenty institutions joined in this project: (1) Students, faculty, and administrators design and develop the program. (2) A broad mix of resources—including regular courses, research assistantships, internships, field experience, independent study, individual and group projects, telelectures, video tapes, programmed learning, and travel—is to be used. (3) There is no fixed curriculum and no fixed time for the award of a degree. (4) A broad age range (16 to 60 or older) is included. (5) Adjunct faculty—government officials, business executives, scientists, artists, writers—is used. (6) Continuing dialogue be-

External Degree Programs

tween students and faculty is maintained—by means of student-advisor meetings, seminars, correspondence, teleconferences, and the like. (7) Seminars are devoted to the development of skills for independent learning. (8) Programs and resources of other UWW participants are open to all. (9) Each student must produce a "Major Contribution": a research study, work of art, a book, a publishable article. (10) Achievement of graduates is to be researched.

The example of the modes-of-learning model which has attracted the most attention recently is the British Open University. In fact, so great has been the flow of visitors to this institution that it is becoming a mark of distinction among American educators to be able to say that one has not visited the Open University.

The first year's applicant group (summer 1970) to Open University exceeded 42,000 for 25,000 places. In the summer of 1971, more than 35,000 applications were received for 21,000 student places. Selection is essentially on a first-come, first-served basis, except that there are quotas for course, region, and occupation. About 25 per cent of the applicants in 1971 wished to take two courses, as compared to 45 per cent in 1970 (Open University, *Analysis,* 1971).

Open University illustrates the modes-of-learning model because this institution has designed a special curriculum for the adult audience (all students are over 21 years of age) that the program is to attract. Recognizing that it is dealing with an adult population, Open University schedules the pace and amount of its instruction on the assumption that its students have other full-time responsibilities. Instruction is broken into segments, which are to be completed in a prescribed sequence. Evaluations of the students' progress are made at the conclusion of each major segment, and the students who are successful are credited with having accomplished that segment. While end-of-course examinations are used, credit for having

106

completed the course is also determined by evaluations of the students' work throughout the course. The degree will be awarded upon successful completion of the prescribed courses of the program. Student progress toward the degree is readily apparent, since the courses required for the degree are known and fixed.

> Degree-seeking students have to study not less than ten hours a week and attend either a one-week or two-week summer school, depending on their schedule. The degree is obtained piecemeal, as it is in American undergraduate schools, by accumulating credits in individual courses. The forty-week academic year runs from January to December with a summer break, and each subject course requires a year and includes a terminal examination. Within reason, students are authorized to take as many years as they wish in order to complete an undergraduate or graduate degree.
>
> A system of foundation courses is built into the program. These are offered in four general subjects: literature, culture and society, mathematics, and science. Students are required to satisfy credits in two of these foundation courses before going on to an advanced level, where courses are offered in sixteen or more special subjects and where they may take subjects unrelated to their foundation courses. Each subject is divided into two stages, each stage being the subject of a year's course and constituting one credit. Six credits are required for an ordinary undergraduate degree; eight for a more specialized degree.
>
> As far as can be ascertained at this time, the general policy of the Open University will be to keep academic departmentalization to a minimum. Most students will

be encouraged to take courses in differing areas in making up their programs; thus, the direction appears to be toward the identification of fundamental principles and broad concepts and a feeling for the unity and general composition of knowledge in the subject areas. This new university would seem to be encouraging the student to increase his learning ability by helping him to understand the subject in a way that will enable him to relate other information to it. In effect, it stresses the interrelationships of the various subject fields offered and attempts to reestablish a sense of the unity of knowledge.

From the very beginning Open University faculty groups have been engaged in curriculum planning with a wide range of alternatives and a diversity of general objectives related to the liberal education of adults. In the process, they have sought to offer their students an array of learning experiences and to unite living and learning so as to produce as perfect and complete a human being as possible. Essentially, the Open University rejects conventional patterns and is starting from scratch with a new curriculum, a new concept, and a new faculty [Lester, 1971, pp. 8–9].

The modes-of-learning model may share with the administrative-facilitation model the use of technology and the provision of special student services. Open University, for example, has specially prepared texts and workbooks geared to an independent learner studying at home, instruction beamed to the student's home at convenient hours via radio and television, learning centers where the student can receive televised instruction should he not have access to a private receiver, inexpensive kits that permit students to conduct scientific experiments at home, and tutors at locations convenient to the student to provide assistance if needed. Open University's use of such techniques in common with their use by institutions cited as examples of the administrative-facilitation model should not lead to a confusion of these two models. For example, Open University and Stanford in the master's degree program in engineering both televise instruction to off-campus students. However, Stanford holds to its customary degree pattern whereas Open University has designed a new curriculum and a new degree pattern for the students it serves.

Another recent proposal has been offered by Lawrence Dennis, Provost and Director of the Massachusetts State College System. Dennis (1971) has called for the establishment of a University of North America—a confederation of junior and senior colleges and universities and other educational associations and agencies. The University of North America would arrange for the delivery of college-degree-level instructional programs to adults via television supplemented by radio, correspondence studies, films, programmed instruction, libraries, theaters, museums, tutorials, conferences, and seminars at regional learning institutes. The University of North America would marshall educational resources and facilities in Canada and Mexico as well as the United States.

Dennis indicates that his proposal is directed primarily to the adult learner, but he does not specify whether traditional or new degree patterns would prevail. Hence, it is not possible to determine whether the proposal should be classified under the administrative-facilitation model or the modes-of-learning model.

EXAMINATION MODEL

The third model of an external degree, the examination model, is about to become operational in the United States. In this model an institution or agency which need not itself offer instruction leading to an external degree awards credits and degrees on the basis of student performance as evidenced by examination. The program being readied for introduction in this country is the plan of the New York State Education Department (1970, 1971) to offer a Regents Baccalaureate Degree. The announced timetable for the New York plan calls for the first candidates to be examined and degrees awarded to the successful candidates in 1972. The candidate will be able to earn his degree exclusively on the basis of examination performance. Both oral and written examinations will be used. Evidently the first opportunity to qualify for such a degree will be in the field of business adminstration. Continued development of the program will lead to opportunities for degrees in other fields and at the associate level at a later time.

Under the New York plan faculty members of regular colleges and universities will play a pivotal role in determining the kinds of examinations to be used and the standards to be set for degree qualifications. In addition, to assist in the establishment of reasonable standards for non-traditional students, the examinations will first be tried out on regular college students just before they receive their degrees.

The examination model, of course, has a world-renowned illustration in the University of London. Since 1858 external students (individuals not enrolled in one of the constituent colleges of the University) have been permitted to take the regular examinations required of internal students. Successful performance on these examinations leads to the University of London degree.

There are matriculation requirements for external students as well as internal students at the University of London. In fact, its matriculation requirements for external candidates are set at or above those established for internal students. For example, "From 1962 external students reading for the B.Sc.

John R. Valley

Economics have been required to obtain passes in three advanced-level subjects, two at Grade D, at one sitting, or some other combination of results held to be equivalent. (This compares, essentially, with a normal requirement of two advanced-level passes.)" (Duke, 1967, p. 6). Candidates for the University of London degree are not left to their own devices to prepare for the degree. Students are prepared for the examinations through colleges that offer courses leading to a University of London degree. In addition, private or proprietary correspondence instruction is available to assist external students.

Depending upon the specific degree being pursued by the candidate, the expected preparation for the examinations is different. External candidates for the B.D., B.A., L.Lb., B.Mus., and B.Sc. (in the faculties of science and economics) may prepare for the examination without restriction. They may be instructed in teaching institutions in London that are not part of the university, in institutions elsewhere in the United Kingdom, or overseas. They may also prepare by private study. On the other hand, external candidates for the M.B., B.S., B.Ds., and B.Sc. (in the faculty of engineering) are expected to pursue approved courses of study in institutions recognized by the University of London. Candidates for other University of London external degrees have similar special requirements. For advanced degrees external candidates are expected to possess a degree from the University of London in the appropriate faculty.

The external degree programs of the University of London are substantial operations. In 1967–68, 3,258 external degrees were awarded as compared to 9,003 internal degrees. Of the total external degrees, 3,061 were first degrees, 64 were master's degrees and 133 were doctoral degrees (*Commonwealth Universities Yearbook*, 1970, p. 369).

Although the University of London and the New York State Regents degrees are both examples of the examination model, these examples differ in several important respects. First, the University of London degree is open only to matriculated students. Hence, admission to degree candidacy is highly selective. Apparently, New York degree candidates will not be screened. Second, the degree-granting authority in the one instance is a university that normally enrolls students; in the other instance, although it is an agency of university status (The University of the State of New York), it does not normally enroll students. Third, while the University of London presumably is worldwide in the candidates it attracts, it probably serves individuals who have been nurtured in the British educational tradition. The geographic scope of the New York Regents degree, while it cannot be determined at this point, may be more limited.

Other recent proposals for external degrees also illustrate the examination model. Hugh McKean (1969), Chancellor of Rollins College, has suggested that a National College be established to award degrees on the basis of achievement demonstrated on rigorous examinations. Lieberman and Wycoff (1970) have suggested that Educational Testing Service be empowered by federal or state charters to offer degrees exclusively on the basis of examination performance. Presumably, according to their plan, the examinations would be open to anyone who wished to take them and the degree would be awarded to those who qualify via examinations. In addition to the University of London, other institutions that may not be as well known to American audiences that offer external degrees via examinations are the University of Ceylon, the University of Burdwan, and the University of Calcutta.

Where institutions have established their normal degree requirements in terms of examinations rather than courses, apparently it would be rather simple to implement an external degree of the examination model. All that need be done would be to open eligibility to the degree-qualifying examinations to nonresidential students. Whether any American colleges or universities which have established their degree requirements in terms of examination will open the door to external students remains to be seen.

Specific instances of external degree programs or proposals in the examination model may differ in particular features. For example, admissions policies may range from open admissions to highly selective matriculation; degrees may be awarded by established regular institutions or by new institutions especially created for this purpose; degrees may be awarded by teaching institutions or by nonteaching institutions; institutions may be state-based, or national, or even international in scope; degrees may be awarded by public or by privately controlled institutions; degrees may be based on local teacher-made examinations or on examinations produced by professional measurement experts. These features by no means exhaust the dimensions along which differences might occur. However, this presentation would become needlessly complex if an attempt were made to take each of these dimensions as a basis for developing a different examination model for an external degree.

VALIDATION MODEL

In the validation model, an institution or agency evaluates the student's total learning experiences from whatever means. It evaluates this total learning experience in terms of its conception of a degree and indicates any additional requirements needed. When they have been met, it awards the degree. The institution authorized to award a degree is presumed to have a clear set of degree requirements and a willingness to permit completion of its requirements by a variety of means. It need not, of course, follow the validation model for all of its students. It might limit this path to a degree to, say, adults over some arbitrary age.

The validation model could operate somewhat as follows. The student, with the assistance of the participating institution, would assemble a full record of his educational achievement to date. This compilation could include transcripts of courses completed in regular colleges or universities, results of examinations of college-level achievement, transcripts of courses taken in the military and supported by recommendations of the Commission on Accreditation of Service Experiences, courses taken at places of business, and correspondence courses. All of these records would be compared against a set of degree requirements and determinations made as to what requirements had been met. The candidate would be directed to any remaining requirements, and he might be assisted in meeting these requirements by equally varied means—regular courses, independent study followed by examinations, correspondence courses, or any other feasible method.

The Westbrook plan (Westbrook College, Portland, Maine) closely approximates this model. Westbrook College operates as a junior college; however, it is authorized to award baccalaureate degrees. The plan permits two-year graduates of Westbrook to qualify for a Westbrook bachelor's degree by completing the additional requirements elsewhere. When the student submits evidence to Westbrook that an agreed-upon degree program has been completed, Westbrook awards the degree (*Maine Sunday Telegram,* 1970; Westbrook College, *Announcing the Westbrook Plan*).

It seems likely that the Bloomfield College Contract Program, initiated in the fall of 1971, will exemplify the validation model. Complete information was not available about the new program at the time this report was prepared. However, in a letter dated September 20, 1971, President Allshouse listed the principal features of the program:

John R. Valley

(1) There is and should be no standard route for achieving a liberal education; thus, our first question for a prospective candidate is, Why do you want a liberal-arts education and what skills and qualities of mind and person are you seeking? (2) A contract is not a euphemism for a rearrangement of the regular B.A. requirements. Rather, it is an opportunity to present work service and volunteer experiences as not simply the equivalent of standard courses, but as valid foundations for demonstrating the qualities which characterize the educated person. (3) Our college is a place where learning experiences should be organized —not localized. Hence, there is no prescribed residence requirement for any Contract Program.

A proposal that illustrates the validation model is the plan of the Academy for Educational Development (1971), which calls for the establishment of an International University for Independent Study (IUIS). This new degree-granting institution would establish patterns or sets of degree requirements, and it would be prepared to accept a variety of evidence testifying to completion of these requirements. This evidence might include successful completion of correspondence courses, performance on the College-Level Examination Program, Advanced Placement Examinations, New York Proficiency Examinations, completion of courses in the military, or completion of regular college courses. In keeping with its name, International University for Independent Study would be worldwide in scope. Initially it will conduct its operations in English, but ultimately is expected to serve candidates with other language backgrounds as well.

Attention is called to another common practice that approximates the validation model, but this practice focuses attention on the early or beginning rather than the final steps toward degree qualification. Through the granting of credit as well as placement, entering students at many institutions may obtain course credit which counts toward their total degree requirements. This credit is given on the basis of national examinations or locally devised tests, or interviews, or the submission of other evidence of achievement for evaluation. Since 1956 the Advanced Placement Program has served more than 430,000 secondary school candidates, who have taken approximately 570,000 examinations. The results of these examinations are transmitted to the college of the student's choice, and if the student's performance is at a level that satisfies his college, the student is awarded credit toward the completion of degree requirements. Since the typical Advanced Placement candidates submit scores for only one or two courses, for them the program does not materially alter the ways in which they meet degree requirements. However, some students take sufficient Advanced Placement courses and examinations to qualify for a year or more of undergraduate credit on the basis of studies completed external to their degree awarding institution.

The Advanced Placement Program, being concerned with introductory or beginning college-level work, results in credit for early rather than final degree requirements. More recently the College-Level Examination Program (CLEP) has broadened this approach to meeting degree requirements. CLEP argues for the award of credit without concern for any formal study; for widening the population to be served to include anyone, not just recent secondary school graduates; and for providing achievement examinations in areas and courses not served by the Advanced Placement Program. By 1971 about 850 colleges and universities have indicated that they are prepared to grant college course credit to successful CLEP candidates.

CREDITS MODEL

The credits model of an external degree can be described as follows: An institution or agency that does not itself offer instruction awards credits and degrees for which it sets standards and vouches for the quality of student programming. There is no American operational illustration of this model. An agency does exist that performs some functions of this model, but it does so for a restricted population. The Commission on Accreditation of Service Experiences (CASE) of the American Council on Education makes recommendations for the awarding of college credit for instruction completed in the military service. Its recommendations are based on reviews of the military service courses by consultants, civilian educators who are experts in the academic areas concerned. The recommendations of these educators are published in a guide (Turner, 1968) which CASE distributes to all colleges and universities. The guide identifies the military course by title(s), location, and length. It includes a statement of the objectives of the course and its coverage, and finally it gives the credit recommendations at the collegiate level. These recommendations are for junior college, baccalaureate, and graduate credits; and the recommendation includes both the amount of credit and the course for which credit might be granted (for instance, "three semester hours in cost accounting and three semester hours in government accounting"). In addition, CASE has an advisory service to offer recommendations to college officials for courses that may not be included in the published guide.

Several changes would be necessary in CASE's operations before it could illustrate the credits model of an external degree. First, CASE currently is confined to making recommendations. To conform to the model, CASE would need to acquire the authority not simply to recommend but actually to award college or university course credit. Second, CASE's authority is limited to instruction offered by the military. To embrace the model more fully, CASE might include proprietary correspondence instruction or perhaps instruction offered by private industry (courses offered by IBM, the Life Office Management Association, or the American Institute of Banking, among others). Third, CASE is currently acting on behalf of military personnel or former military personnel. To approximate the model, CASE might serve civilians as well as the military. Finally, CASE now deals only with course credits rather than degrees. So to match the model CASE would need to extend its awards to include full degrees.

We need, therefore, to turn to England to find an actual example of the *credits* model in operation.* The Council for National Academic Awards (CNAA) was established by royal charter in 1964 to administer degrees and other awards to students in Great Britain in approved courses of degree standard outside the universities. The council consists of representatives of the regional and area colleges involved, as well as industrial interests. The colleges themselves are not authorized to award degrees. CNAA is not an examining body, but it awards degrees on the basis of examinations drawn up by the colleges providing the courses. "Its charter requires that the standards of these degrees should be comparable with that of university degrees. . . . Such has been the pace of CNAA's activities and the response of the colleges to the opportunities presented that there are today over 20,000 students following

* A note in the section of the *Commonwealth Universities Yearbook 1970* (p. 10) dealing with Australian institutions indicates that the state of Victoria has established the Victoria Institute of Colleges—an organization that will have the power to award degrees for courses of university standard. While this new organization appears to parallel CNAA, I have been unable to obtain further information about its operation. It is therefore cited as a possible—but as yet unconfirmed—second example.

CNAA courses . . . in some seventy subjects" (Department of Education and Science and the Central Office of Information, 1970, p. 3). In 1970 forty-nine colleges reportedly were offering CNAA courses (*Commonwealth Universities Yearbook*, 1970, p. 126). The council awards degrees at the undergraduate and graduate level including the doctorate.

CNAA has a permanent staff of about thirty. However, it involves a substantial cadre of professional and technical people who serve on its various boards and commissions. The council's annual budget is about £150,000, contributed to by each student at the public colleges as part of his fees. Courses offered by the colleges and polytechnics that participate in the council are validated for about a five- or six-year period (Summerskill, 1971).

To my knowledge there is no direct parallel of this model either extant or among the recent American proposals for external degrees.

COMPLEX-SYSTEMS MODEL

The descriptions of the five models earlier in this paper cover most but not all of the known or proposed external degree programs. An additional model is needed in order to be all-inclusive. Thus, we have the complex-systems model: A degree-granting institution or agency reshapes its pattern of services in various ways, sometimes by combining various simpler models of external degree programs so as to meet the needs of a different clientele. When various external degree models are combined with one another, it is more appropriate to think of the result as an external degree system rather than an external degree program. Several proposals illustrate this approach.

One is a proposal (Arbolino and Valley, 1970) calling for the establishment of a national university to offer external degrees based on the examination, credits, and validation models. This national university would not itself engage in teaching but would work cooperatively and intensively with regular colleges and universities and utilize their instructional resources for external degree purposes.

Regarding degrees, the national university would function in three ways. First, it would itself award degrees—at the associate, baccalaureate, and graduate-professional levels—based on examinations. Second, it would award degrees jointly with regular colleges and universities when a substantial portion (for instance, more than half) of the degree requirements had been met by national university credits. Third, when its credits were recognized by colleges and universities, it would facilitate degree completion at these institutions.

The function of the national university in the awarding of credit is regarded as an important one. Currently, individuals bring to colleges and universities exceedingly diverse statements of educational accomplishment: test scores, empolyment histories, military service records, certificates issued by proprietary schools, volunteer service statements, correspondence course completions. At many institutions there is a basic attitude that favors recognizing all previous accomplishment. The barriers reside in the complexity of doing so with justice to both the individual and the institution. Since the resources that individual institutions can bring to these problems are limited, there is need for an agency to approach these matters systematically. The proposed national university could serve this function.

Further, the national university would award credit for successful completion of programs of instruction outside traditional institutions of higher education—proprietary, military, foreign, correspondence, industrial, and so forth—without invariably resorting to the technique of validating examinations.

120

John R. Valley

Whenever the national university was invited to do so by an agency offering instruction on a continuing basis, it would review the work in question. This review would be accomplished by a panel of experts who, if they were satisfied that the work offered represented college-level instruction, would recommend the amount and level of national university credit. When the preceding step had been accomplished, individuals who submitted documentary evidence of having successfully completed a national university accredited course would receive national university credit.

A registry of educational accomplishment would be the mechanism whereby the national university would achieve the services described above. That is, the university would take diverse statements of individual achievement and convert them into credits. The registry would maintain a continuing record of an individual's achievement, and it would be prepared to transmit this record upon the request of the individual to employers or to educational institutions where he planned to engage in further study.

Space limitations prohibit discussion of other functions of this national university. Such additional functions, however, would include the following: encouraging the development and use of all instructional resources for external degree purposes; assisting students who wish to transfer; providing advisory and consulting services on continuing education for employers; maintaining a program of research and development supportive of continuing education; providing the examinations and other services necessary to the implementation of the national university; maintaining a forum, including publications devoted to the development of continuing education.

Although Arbolino and Valley were reaching for an organization that would be national in scope, their plan could

121

be implemented more modestly, perhaps on a state or regional level or by a consortium of like-minded traditional institutions, if this were seen as politically more viable or desirable.

Another example of the complex-systems model proposed at the state level is that developed by a group working at the University of Wisconsin under the direction of Charles A. Wedemeyer. A paper entitled "The Open Education System" (Wisconsin Governor's Task Force, 1970) contains a description of the system, a design for its management, and indications of the ways it could function. The system proposed in this instance does not focus exclusively at the college level but concerns itself with children, including preschoolers, as well as adults. The Open Education System would have a governing board on a par with the four other educational governing boards of the state. The Open Education Board would establish and develop a Learning Resources Center to coordinate and organize those extension services applicable to the Open Education System, establish and develop a Communications Resources Center to coordinate and organize the communications and media resources needed by the Open Education System, and establish an Open School to serve as the program development and delivery unit of the Open Education System.

Another recently implemented example of the complex-systems model external degree is Empire State College (Empire State College, *The New Non-residential College;* Farber, 1971; *State University of New York News,* March 8, 1971, and September 13, 1971). This new institution in the state of New York is designed to serve a nonresidential student body and will provide a variety of services. It will offer screening and testing to help establish a student's proper entry level if something beyond beginning freshman courses would be appropriate. It will have learning centers throughout the state to provide counseling; maintain records; and offer library resources and instructional services, including correspondence courses. The New York Educational Television Network also will be utilized.

Empire State College will have an administrative staff and a faculty but no campus in the traditional sense. It plans to offer the Associate in Arts, Bachelor of Arts, Bachelor of Arts in an interdisciplinary area, and Bachelor of Arts in an academic major degree. The degrees will be conferred by the State University of New York. The student may use any number of means to qualify for his degree: independent study; studies prepared by the college faculty and offered via various technologies and media; studies completed at one of the seventy units of the state university; examinations; credits for employment, research, or community service. Full-time students would pay the standard tuition of $550, and they could expect to complete the requirements for the associate degree in two years and the baccalaureate degree in four years. Part-time study will also be possible.

Utilizing faculty from the New York State School of Industrial and Labor Relations at Cornell University, a Labor College Division was established in Manhattan as the first Learning Center of Empire State College in the fall of 1971. This unit serves the needs of labor unions and executives. The New York City Central Labor Council provides physical facilities for the Center and contributes to its operating expenses. The Labor College Division in its bachelor's degree program includes technical training offered by unions and industry and on-the-job experiences; professional studies in areas related to students' career plans; and liberal-arts studies. Programs are planned for about 200 students.

Empire State College also needs to be considered in conjunction with the New York Regents Degree. The former can be seen essentially as an instructional delivery system which could work in tandem with the New York Regents Degree program. Thus, Empire State College might provide some or all

123

of the instruction needed by candidates pursuing the New York Regents Degree.

There are some preliminary indications that complex-systems external degrees are also being considered within the California University System and the California State College System. An interesting project (entitled *The External Degree Project*) has been undertaken by the Policy Institute of the Syracuse University Research Corporation. Working with public and private universities and colleges, as well as the State Education Department, The Policy Institute hopes to develop a design for an external degree program in the five New York counties of Cayuga, Cortland, Madison, Onondaga, and Oswego. Among the issues to be confronted are such matters as the sponsorship of the external degree program, collaboration with existing activities, ways of getting local and civic support, the need for awards other than degrees, and the financing of the external degree program.

Finally, at the ACE 1971 annual meeting in Washington, D.C., a plan for the Video University was described (Mood, 1971). This new institution, perhaps a federally chartered national university or a consortium of existing universities, would make available a vast array of instructional materials on video cassettes; maintain a computerized catalog of these materials; offer computerized testing of student progress; design external degree programs and award degrees; and utilize television networks to disseminate information about learning and career opportunities. The proponent believes that after an initial capitalization the institution would support itself from cassette rental fees, fees to use the computer network and catalog, test fees, and transcript fees.

CONCLUSIONS

While I have not conducted a comprehensive survey of existing models or recent proposals, the information that has

John R. Valley

come to my attention as analyzed in the preceding pages leads to the following conclusions:

First, regarding the administrative-facilitation model, while the exact number of programs among American institutions that fit this model is not known, the model is a fairly common and widespread one. Second, regarding the modes-of-learning model, illustrations of this model are also fairly common. This model together with the administrative-facilitation model has been the basis for the design of most programs directed to the service of adult populations. Third, the remaining models of external degree programs and systems have not been implemented with the same frequency. The examination model is only now about to become operational in the United States; the validation model is almost nonexistent despite the fact that it would appear to be relatively easy to implement; and the credits model can be illustrated only by a non-American example. But, with the American propensity for the big picture and the grand design, complex-systems models seem currently to be attracting the attention of many planners in this country particularly within state educational systems.

REFERENCES

Academy for Educational Development. *Proposed Establishment of the International University for Independent Study.* New York: Academy for Educational Development, February 1, 1971. (Mimeo.)

ARBOLINO, J. N., AND VALLEY, J. R. "Education: The Institution or the Individual." *Continuing Education,* 1970, *3*(4), 6, 55.

Commonwealth Universities Yearbook 1970. London: Association of Commonwealth Universities, 1970.

DENNIS, L. E. *"Other End of Sesame Street."* In G. K. Smith (Ed.), *New Teaching, New Learning: Current Issues in Higher Education 1971.* San Francisco: Jossey-Bass, 1971.

Department of Education and Science and the Central Office of Information. *After "A" Levels.* London, 1970.

Department of Housing and Urban Development. *Basic Information on HUD's University Without Walls: National Urban Studies Program.* Washington, D.C.: HUD, Community Development Training Program, December 11, 1970. (Mimeo.)

DUKE, C. *The London External Degree and the English Part-Time Degree Student.* Leeds: University Press, 1967.

Empire State College. *The New Non-residential College of the State University of New York: Some Questions and Answers.* Undated.

FARBER, M. A. "State Will Open College Without a Campus in Fall," *New York Times,* July 9, 1971, p. 1.

LESTER, R. I. "Britain's University of the Second Chance," *American Education,* 1971, 7(7), 8–9.

LIEBERMAN, B., AND WYCOFF, D. *National Baccalaureate Examinations. A Proposal for a Drastic Change in the Conduct of Undergraduate Education.* Research Memorandum SP-117.1. Pittsburgh: University of Pittsburgh, Departments of Psychology and Sociology, March 1970.

Maine Sunday Telegram. "Westbrook College Reveals Plan to Utilize Transfer Phenomenon," November 8, 1970.

MC KEAN, H. F. "Proposal for Making College-Level Work and Bachelor Degrees Available to All Floridians," *Educational Media,* 1969, 1(7).

MOOD, A. M. "Another Approach to Higher Education." In *Universal Higher Education Costs and Benefits.* Background papers for participants in 1971 annual meeting of American Council on Education, Washington, D. C., October 6–8, 1971. Pp. 169–186.

New York State Education Department. *The New York State Regents Baccalaureate Degree.* Albany, N.Y.: State Education Department, August 18, 1970. (Mimeo.)

New York State Education Department. *External Degrees: Expanding Educational Opportunities for the Independent*

John R. Valley

Learner. Albany, N.Y.: State Education Department, March 1, 1971. (Mimeo.)

Open University. *Analysis of Applications and Allocation of Places for 1972 Courses.* Bletchley, England: Open University, August 13, 1971. (Mimeo.)

Policy Institute, Syracuse University Research Corporation. *The External Degree Project.* Syracuse, N.Y., no date.

State University of New York News. "University Establishes Empire State College," March 8, 1971, p. 1.

State University of New York News. "Empire State College Establishes First Learning Center in Manhattan," September 13, 1971, pp. 1, 6.

SUMMERSKILL, J. "Summary, Visit to Institutions of Higher Learning in England." New York: Office of External Degree Plans, College Entrance Examination Board, 1971.

TRAVERS, J. L. "A Study of Adult Degree Programs in Selected American Colleges and Universities." Unpublished doctoral dissertation, Department of Educational Administration, University of Utah, May 1969.

TURNER, C. P. (Ed.) *A Guide to the Evaluation of Educational Experiences in the Armed Forces.* Washington, D.C.: American Council on Education, 1968.

Union for Experimenting Colleges and Universities. *University Without Walls, Summary Statement: A Proposal for an Experimental Degree Program in Undergraduate Education.* Yellow Springs, Ohio: Antioch College, 1971.

University of South Florida. *Accent on Learning.* General Catalog of the University of South Florida, 1969–70 Bulletin of the University of South Florida. Tampa: University of South Florida, 1969.

University of South Florida. *Bachelor of Independent Studies Adult Degree Program.* Tampa: University of South Florida, undated.

Westbrook College. *Announcing the Westbrook Plan, the "Two*

Plus You" Concept. Portland, Maine: Westbrook College, undated.

Wisconsin Governor's Task Force. *A Forward Look.* Final Report of the Governor's Commission on Education. Madison, 1970.

Index

129

Index

American Council on Education, 24, 117, 124
American Library Association, 59
American Psychological Association, 77
Aptitude versus achievement, 34
ARBOLINO, J. N., 91, 119–121
Arithmetic tests, 74
Armed forces. *See* Military
Attrition, student, 32–33
Australia, external degree in, 100

B

Barrier: of accumulated credits, 45–46; financial, 48; mobility, 43–44; restricted definition of education as, 48–49; to traditional education, 43–49
Bloomfield College Contract Program, 114
Boards, professional licensing, 67
Brigham Young University, 100
BRUNER, J., 15
Business, educational role of, 6, 55–57

C

California Achievement Tests, 74
Campus, residence on, 5, 45
Carnegie Commission on Higher Education, 90
Carnegie Corporation, 2, 58, 97
Certification: economic benefits of, 28–29; of intelligence, 34; of learning, 13, 15, 28, 33, 66, 81–82; by nonacademic agencies, 67, 83, 91; occupational, 50; by one academic institution, 45; various means of, 36. *See also* Evaluation, Recognition

Chemistry tests, 73
Chicago Junior College System, 99
Classroom, 45
CLEP. *See* College-Level Examination Program
College education, meaning of, 12–13. *See also* Traditional education
College Entrance Examination Board, 25, 73–74, 80, 97; Commission on Tests of, 37
College-Level Examination Program, 19, 24–25, 46, 74–75, 80, 85, 115; in Dallas program, 61; external degree via, 116; General Exams of, 67; as used by business, 56–57
College Placement Tests, 73
COLLINS, J. W., 44
Colorado State University, 99
Commission on Accreditation of Service Experiences, 45, 114, 117
Communications: from students, 59–61; to students, 53–59
Communications network, 60–61
Community-based education centers, 25–26
Community college, 49, 58–59
Continuing education, 15. *See also* Adults
Cooperative Examinations, 73–75
Correspondence study, 6, 14, 27; as external degree model, 100; in military, 19, 45
Council for National Academic Awards (England), 118
Counseling, 9, 52; of adults, 57; by armed forces, 55; by business and industry, 55–57; centers for, 26–27;

Index

ness, 55–57; people's knowledge of, 52–59; spread of, 11, 51; student role in designing, 60. *See also* Access

Educational Policy Research Center, 41

Educational Testing Service, 71, 73–75; as degree granter, 112

Elitism, 4

Empire State College, 122–123

Employed people, problems of, 4, 47–48

England, external degree in, 118

Equality. *See* Access, Educational opportunity

Error, measurement, 35–36

Evaluation: of achievement versus aptitude, 34; as anchored to instruction, 34; coordination of, 89; by criterion-referenced or absolute standards tests, 35, 78, 87; as dictating curriculum, 35; as different from recognition, 67–68; different models of, 36; of diverse learning experiences, 13; error in, 35–36; expense of, 71; by experts and scholars, 29, 88; by external exam, 33, 72–77; by faculty, 29, 36, 69–72, 88; flexibility in, 37; and general intelligence measures, 34; holistic, 70; individualized, 35; multiple, 35; of non-traditional learning, 9, 32–33, 84–89; normative (standardized), 33, 35, 77, 86; by panels of experts, 88; by performance measures, 87–88; purpose of, 31–32; setting for, 71; study of,

86; subjective, 69; system of, 85; of traditional college learning, 68–78; traditional versus non-traditional, 31; of uncommon subjects, 87; using technological aids, 88; validity, reliability, and practicality of, 70–71, 84

Evening college, 98

Exams. *See* Evaluation, Tests

Expense of non-traditional study, 16–17

Extension courses, 19, 53

External degree, 4; administrative-facilitation model of, 97–100; in California, 124; complex-systems model of, 119–124; by correspondence, 100; credits model for, 117–119; at Empire State College, 122; examination model for, 103, 109–113; modes-of-learning model of, 100–109; at National University, 120; of National Urban Studies Program, 104–105; in Open Education System, 122; at Open University, 106–109; programs for, 95–125; recognition of, 32, 66, 90; technological aids for, 99–100, 105, 108–109, 125; at University Without Walls, 105–106; validation model of, 113–116

External exams, 72–77

F

Faculty: adjunct, 105; caste system among, 2; evaluation by, 29, 36, 69–72, 96; exams for prospective, 75;

Index

receptivity to non-traditional study of, 3; recruitment and evaluation of, 30–31; research of, 31; role in designing degree exams of, 110; as scholars, 29
Faculty-student contact, cost of, 17n
Faculty-student relationship, 9–10, 17, 31, 103, 106
Financial barriers, 48
Financial problems of higher education, 4, 10
Flexibility, 39; doubts about, 9; in education, 5–6, 8–9, 36–37; individual learning as part of, 8, 37; meaning of, 18; in scheduling, 39, 43
Folklore, 11
Formal educational institutions, 68–78. *See also* Traditional education
Free University, 49
FURNISS, W. T., 19

G

General Educational Development tests, 24
Geographical barriers, 43–44
Government, educational role of, 6, 104–105. *See also* Agencies
Grades, 66, 79
Graduate Record Examinations, 73–74
Guidance. *See* Counseling

H

Halo effect, 36
HEIST, P., 18, 48
HEMBROUGH, B. L., 46, 48
High school equivalency test, 24, 27
HOBAN, C. F., 45

I

ILLICH, I., 15
Independent study, 14, 17n, 103
Individualized learning, 7–8, 16
Industry. *See* Business
Information: clearinghouse for, 58; from community college, 58; from libraries, 59; models for dissemination of, 60–61; network of, 53, 60–61; from and about non-traditional students, 53, 59–61; to non-traditional students, 26–27, 52–59
Inmates, prison, 4, 43–44
Instruction, 34; as educational process, 15; knowledge of sources of, 52–55; questions about, 5; with technological aids, 6, 88, 99–100, 108–109, 124
International University for Independent Study, 115
Interruption of study, 5

J

JOHNSTONE, J. W. C., 41, 44, 47–54

K

Knowledge as power, 40
KNOWLES, M. S., 59
KOERNER, J. D., 82
KREPS, J., 20, 26

L

Labor unions, 6
Language tests, 74–75
Learning: immutable truths about, 5; individualized, 7–8; in institutions, 15–16; lifelong, 40, 51; new skills in, 7; as opposed to schooling, 15; reasons for continued, 50–51

Index

Index

search on, 52; role of various agencies in, 6
NORC study, 41, 44, 47–54
Normative approach to evaluation, 77–78
Nursing, tests of, 73–75
NYQUIST, E. B., 97

O

Occupational reasons for learning, 51
Occupational recognition, 67
OLTMAN, R. M., 48
Open Education System, 122
Open University, British, 33, 97

P

Parallel education system, 4, 6–7
Part-time students, 47–48, 59
Peace Corps, 21, 36
Periphery, educational, 41
Physically handicapped, 43–44
PIFER, A., 97
Placement, student, 81
Planning, educational, 41
Policy Institute of Syracuse University Research Corporation, 124
Practicality of tests, 70–71, 76
Prison inmates, 4, 43–44
Professionals, education for, 4
Programs: counseling in, 60; development of, 105; external degree, 95–125; for people, 49–52, 60
Proprietary schools, 6
Psychological Corporation, 73, 85

Q

Quality: and accreditation, 82; concern for, 8–9, 29–30, 65; and credibility, 32;

maintaining, 13; versus quantity of education, 28
Quality control, 29–30

R

Radcliffe Institute for Independent Study, 58
Reading tests, 74
Recognition, 9; academic, 66; by academic credit, 13; as different from evaluation, 67; of external degree, 66; flexibility in, 37; forms of, 66, 68, 79, 90, 95; grades as, 79–80; and manpower needs, 92; at national university registry, 121; by nonacademic agencies, 67, 91–92; of nonschool experiences, 21; of non-traditional study, 89–92; occupational, 67, 90–91; problems of, 64–93; as related to employment, 28–29; reserved to institutions, 95–96; and selection and screening of students, 66; social benefits of, 92; standards of, 66, 95–96; of traditional college learning, 79–84, 93, 95–96; worth of, 79. *See also* Certification, Credit, Degree(s), Evaluation
Registry of educational accomplishment, 121
Reliability of tests, 70–72, 76
Research, need for, 10, 52, 60
Residence requirements, 5, 19–20
Retired people, 4
RIVERA, R. J., 41, 44, 47–54

S

Scheduling problems, 43, 47–48
Schooling as opposed to education, 15

135

Index

Index

United States Department of Housing and Urban Development, 104
University of Detroit, 105
University of London, 32, 110–112
University of North America, 109
University of Northern Colorado, 105
University of Oklahoma, 100, 105
University of South Carolina, 99
University of South Florida, 100–104
University Without Walls, 26, 60, 104–106
Utah system of service centers, 61

V

Validity of tests, 70–71, 76
VALLEY, J. R., 91, 119–121
Veterans, 4, 46

Video University, 124
VISTA, 21, 36
Vocational education, 4, 51

W

WEBB, E., 35
WEDEMEYER, C. A., 122
WEISBERG, R., 44
Westbrook plan, 114
WHITE, M. S., 58
WILLINGHAM, W. W., 43–44, 54
WILSON, R., 18
WITMER, D. R., 28
Women students, 4; concessions for, 48; counseling of, 57–58; financial problems of, 47–48; mobility problems of, 20, 46; scheduling problems of, 47–48
Work experience, 6
WYKOFF, D., 112